PUB WALKS
A R O U N D
PORTSMOUTH
& THE SOUTH DOWNS

Ensign
PUBLICATIONS

JOHN PRICE

First published in 1991
by **Ensign Publications**
a division of Hampshire Books Ltd.,
2 Redcar Street
Southampton SO1 5LL

a

ISBN 185455 070 5

Publisher: *David Graves*
Cover Photo: *Terry Heathcote*
Cover Design: *The Design Lab*
Text pages: *PageMerger*
Maps & design: *The Precinct Press*
Printers: *MRM Assoc. Ltd., Reading*

Pubberstamp
© John Price & Hampshire Books Ltd.,
1991

CIP data available from British Library

· INTRODUCTION ·

This life at best is but an inn,
And we the passengers (James Howell)

In this book you will find walks for all seasons and all moods. The walks have been chosen for two reasons: they take you through some of the best scenery that the area has to offer; and they all start from the oldest, unspoilt country pubs and inns that I have been able to find.

Each walk has been independently tested to ensure as far as is possible that the directions are error free. Also, if the right of way has appeared at all in doubt, then I have obtained confirmation from the Rights of Way Officer of the respective county council. I can therefore say, hand on heart, that everything possible has been done to ensure accuracy at the time of going to press. You can therefore relax in the knowledge that you are walking on confirmed rights of way, where freedom is yours to enjoy and not a soul can legally stop you. .

The most frequent complaint that I hear from walkers is the selfish habit of landowners who plough up footpaths, do not restore them promptly and let crops obscure the way (usually that damnable oilseed rape that is pretty for one week of the summer and pretty awful for the rest). The Rights of Way Act 1990, has changed the law in our favour. Landowners can now only plough if they carry out restorative work within 24 hours of the disturbance or within 14 days if it is the first disturbance for that crop. The surface should be made good and the line of the path should be made apparent; for example, with posts high enough to be seen at all times of the year.

If, when you are abroad in the countryside you come across a transgression, then you should report it to the Rights of Way Officer at either:

Hampshire Recreation Department,   or   County Surveyor's Department,
North Hill Close,   County Hall,
Andover Road,   Tower Street,
Winchester,   Chichester,
Hampshire, SO22 6AQ   West Sussex, PO19 1RL

You should include a six-figure map reference, the nature of the problem and the date.

And now a few words on the pubs. Most of the publicans are happy for walkers to use their car parks providing that they use the pub at the beginning or end of their walk. If you do not wish to visit the pub from where the walk starts and ends (the walks are all circular) then please do not use the pub car park; it is always possible to park somewhere nearby. However, I anticipate that many walkers will want to use the pubs, so to help you plan your walk I have included practical information about the facilities that the pub offers. For example, if children cannot be accommodated because of the lack of a separate room away from the immediate bar, or whether dogs are welcome; in fact, everything that a 'family walker' is likely to want to know.

However I must stress that this is a walking book and not a pub guide. If a walk starts from a village with two pubs, I have tried to mention them both, but I have obviously had to feature one pub in more detail than the other. This does not mean that it is better than its brother, but probably means that it offers greater historical interest. Also, pubs can change their nature overnight if their ownership changes. And, in this day and age with breweries selling off their less profitable pubs, or asking impossible rents from their tenants, we are likely to see frequent changes of ownership or even the closure of some of our best-loved pubs and inns.

At the end of this book you will find a grid. This is for the inveterate collectors among you. Each pub has agreed to hold a rubber stamp and stamp your book when requested, during opening hours. Will you be the first to walk from all twenty-one pubs?

If you have any feedback on this book, comments, criticisms or corrections, I will be very pleased to hear from you via the publisher, whose address is at the front of the book.

Finally, please do not drink and drive and above all enjoy the peace that the countryside brings to us all. Happy walking!

John Price
May 1991

Walk · CONTENTS · Page

· INDEX of PUBS ·

PUBS · and · WALKING

No. Sir, there is nothing which has yet been contrived by man,
by which so much happiness is produced,
as by a good tavern or inn (Samuel Johnson)

A walker's enjoyment of a pub varies according to the time of year. In winter we arrive to leave our muddy boots outside, draw a strong ale, put our wet clothes over the back of a chair, sit in the ingle-nook and listen to the wind howling around the chimney. A pungent mixture of woodsmoke and damp clothes pervades the air as the warmth from the fire melts the cold in our bodies, our muscles at last relax and we take our ease. Just six months later in high summer, we arrive dehydrated and parched, hot and bothered. Boy's beer is the order of the day, or better still perhaps, if we arrive back early in the afternoon, a good pot of strong tea.

Walks should be quiet, unhurried affairs, best enjoyed on one's own, with a friend, or with a few members of the family. There is nothing worse than taking a walk with someone who constantly 'witters', or to walk with someone who thunders along like an express train oblivious of the beauties of the countryside a few feet away. It is not uncommon in the country, to see a score or so of walkers in a long straggly line, more reminiscent of a 'wagon train' than anything else. They can be heard coming from half a mile away; as you stand aside they stride past at a furious pace with no inclination to pass the time of day, and you then hear them for another half a mile as they disappear into the distance. Walking should not be like this; it should be an idle ambling affair. There should be no schedule to keep; no hard and fast plan; no targets except those essential for comfort – in simple terms food, drink and sleep. So, if we have enjoyed our walk the pub is the perfect complement. The warmth and conviviality of a pub to contrast with the solitude of a walk. An opportunity to get to know the people of the country as well as the country itself.

Coming to a pub after a walk, there is no doubt that a walker enjoys his sojourn more than others that have arrived by less noble means, save perhaps the cyclist. After all, the walker is on the moral high ground; he has earned his relaxation, as he comes to a pub by his own efforts and the law allows him to drink as he pleases. The motorist on the other hand, has had an effortless journey and would be well advised to avoid alcohol anyway.

You will not find, located in the pages of this book, or in fact anywhere, a country pub that fits the ideal of the perfect walkers' pub. What you will find are pubs that will welcome the walker – and his boots – and his dog. You will find pubs that have no chromium, no music (excepting that of the live kind) and no fitted carpets. You will find pubs with real ale, real fires, real food and above all, real landlords. There are two rules to be followed when deciding on a pub after a walk. The first one, is always avoid those that appear as well recommended in any *Pub Guide*. These usually sell fizzy beer, and are so busy, that you have to order food at a special hatchway and have your name yelled out at many decibels above that necessary. The second rule is that you should never judge one from the outside as they are often an enigma. The proverb "cold hands, warm heart" is a very appropriate one for the country pub. Inside the most doubtful exterior, the warmest welcome often awaits you.

The closest to the ideal pub that I have encountered, is the one that I am sitting in now. It is set in a valley in the downs, and it is only possible to approach it by a long winding dusty lane, that drops down from the old turnpike road that sweeps through undulating countryside. It is a plain building of humble construction and reputed to be about three-hundred years old. Its white-painted walls reflect the bright spring sunlight and there is a faded sign creaking in the wind. Alongside, is a murky pond, mostly mud, where in recent years, both ducks and water have become rare. You enter through an old arched door that has a vaguely church-like appearance and which takes you into the lower bar. The floor here is made of simple flagstones and is worn smooth by centuries of feet. There is a dartboard in one corner, the day's papers in another and the smell of cooking coming from the kitchen. The only sounds are those of conversation, laughter and pint mugs being filled.

At the back of the room there are some french windows that open outward to a lawn, currently splashed with daffodils – now past their best. The lawn drops away to a footpath at the bottom of the garden, which in turn leads to further unseen footpaths; beyond these, at the foot of the downs, is a field of wheat with waves of wind rippling through it. The downs run as a ridge from left to right, have resisted all attempts at ploughing and are grazed by sheep and rabbits and topped by furze and a considerable amount of hawthorn scrub. To the left, the downs are terminated by a small hanger, or wood, on the side of the hill. Over to the right the odd house is beginning to encroach on the brow of the hill.

This is not a nature reserve, it is ordinary countryside as found in the downland areas of the South Country; an environment gradually produced over the last two or three-thousand years. Within these few square miles, you will find (if you know where to look) a good proportion of all the animal types to be found in England. In spring, the skylark sings overhead, a score of other birds sing their songs, and the house martins perform aerobatic feats under the eaves of the pub.

As night falls in early May, you will, if you are lucky, be able to sit in the garden and hear a nightingale sing from the far hawthorn scrub. To hear these notes on the night air is unforgettable.

An anecdote told by the landlord of this pub, is of a small group of ambitious young salesmen, sitting at a garden table, one evening in May. They spent about an hour or so discussing something that to them was important. It was a warm night and as dusk fell a nightingale began to sing – this stopped their talking. They had not heard one before and were clearly enjoying the beauty of this night song. On the table was a portable telephone that suddenly rang out, disturbing the moment. Without hesitation, the oldest of the three stood up, banged it down hard on the table, and threw it as far as he could over the hedge, away into the field. The landlord maintains that the man walked up the lane, left his job, and was not seen again for over a year; eventually returning and setting up in business as a thatcher. It is a charming story, poignantly contrasting today's pressurised lifestyle with the unhurried beauty of nature.

Old pubs such as this one are in mortal danger as the large breweries look to greater efficiency and a higher return on investment for their shareholders. Hilaire Belloc once wrote that "Inns are the mirror and at the same time the flower of the people". They reflect the nature of our land, and the character of our nation. These same breweries tried to do away with our native beer and homogenise it into a fizzy pasteurised good-for-nothing creation, that nobody really wanted, and then we voted with our feet. The same thing could happen to our country pubs. Let us hope that the same Saxon stubbornness that saved our ale, will also save our country pubs.

But when you have lost your inns
drown your empty selves,
for you will have lost the last of England.
(Hilaire Belloc)

PUB WALKS around
PORTSMOUTH
& the SOUTH DOWNS

1 Harting	8 Bramdean	15 Cocking
2 Compton	9 Owslebury	16 Walderton
3 Chidham	10 Soberton	17 Hawkley
4 Exton	11 Tichborne	18 Elsted
5 Emsworth	12 Charlton	19 Dundridge
6 Finchdean	13 Eartham	20 Chalton
7 Byworth	14 Houghton	21 Hooksway

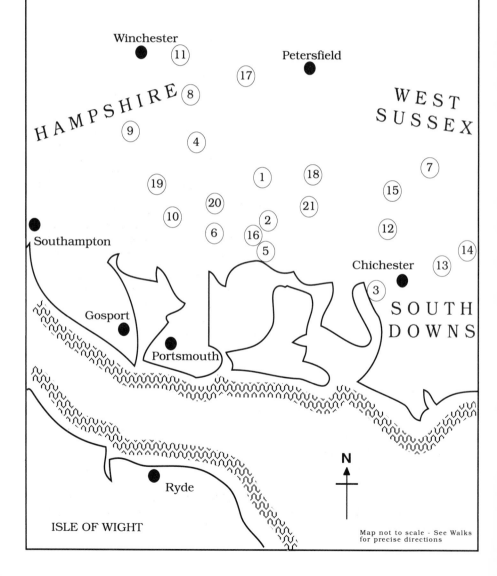

Map not to scale - See Walks
for precise directions

1 · Two Downland Walks from *The White Hart* at South Harting

Background to the Walks

South Harting sits comfortably at the foot of the South Downs; its pale green church spire standing out from the darker green of the downs towering above. The church fits perfectly into its surroundings, being low and large and having that elegant spire.

The village is an ideal place to start a walk: with three fine pubs, a car park, proximity to two long distance footpaths and many other footpaths. It once featured in a promotional film designed to tempt North Americans to come to England – it is not difficult to understand why, as it is a perfect example of a picturesque South Country village; combining the warmth of its attractive, creamy limestone walls with a perfect setting.

As you would expect, an attractive village such as this has featured in the lives and writing of literary figures of past times. Anthony Trollope lived at the Grange (Northend House) during the period 1880-1882. During his career he was very proud of his ability to write a chapter or so before breakfast every day prior to a normal day's work for the Post Office. He also hunted twice a week and lived a very busy social life.

H.P. Gordon who was rector of South Harting wrote a history of his parish in 1877. In this he mentions that Gilbert White (*Natural History of Selborne*) held considerable land in the area at Woodhouse and Nyewood, some at Uppark and at North Marden. He also records the hardship and excesses of the old Sussex field routines that were related to him by an old labourer: "Out in morning at four o'clock. Mouthful of bread and cheese and pint of ale. Then off to the harvest field. Rippin and moen till eight. Then morning brakfast and small beer. Brakfast – a piece of fat pork as thick as your

Map Details
Landranger 1: 50 000
Sheet 197
Pathfinder 1: 25 000
Sheet SU 61/71 and
SU 62/72
Map Reference of
Start/Finish SU785195

Pub Facilities
Food is available at most times and children are made welcome. There is a large, attractive garden in which children may play in the summer. Dogs are only permitted if they are on a lead and not covered in mud! Walkers are welcome to park their cars in the pub car park, providing they patronise the pub before or after their walk. There is a payphone available for customers use. The pub is 'real' – it has real ale and real fires in the winter.

Alternative Facilities
There is the equally good, but not quite so old, Ship Inn. Until recently there was also The Coach and Horses, but I noticed on my last visit to the village that this was closed.

11

How to get there

South Harting is approached using the B2146 from Petersfield. Some parking is possible in the main street and on the short walk it is also possible to park on Harting Hill. The village is served by bus services from Petersfield and Midhurst.

hat is wide. Then work till ten o'clock: then a pint of strong beer (farnooner we called it). Work till twelve. Then at dinner in the farm house; sometimes a leg of mutton, sometimes a piece of ham and plum pudding. Then work till five, then a nunch and a quart of ale. Then work till sunset, then home and have supper and a pint of ale". The rector also records that Harting reputedly had a witch – old Mother Digby who lived at Hog's Lane, East Harting; a woman who apparently had the power to turn herself into a hare and give the hounds a run for their money.

The best day to do one of these walks is Whit Monday (or Spring Bank Holiday Monday as it is now less elegantly known). This is because this particular day sees the annual spring celebration in South Harting – the Harting Festivities. The event is based on the annual celebration of the Harting Old Club;

The White Hart, South Harting.

started in 1800 as Harting Friendly Society.

Many Sussex and Hampshire villages had these clubs (nearby Chalton also had one – see the walks from *The Red Lion* in this book); their general purpose being to provide an insurance against ill health or death before the provision of any form of national insurance or National Health Service. A retirement pension was also provided. A Whit Monday meeting with a parade and feast seems to have been a common feature of all these clubs.

Luckily, the Harting club's history is fairly well recorded over the years of its existence by many writers. The club was formed at a time of hardship generated by the French Wars and a series of disastrous harvests that were to trigger the Labourers' Revolt in the 1830's. In those far off days, the men worked and the women cooked and thus it was, (and still is as far as I know) an organisation for men. Subscriptions were three shillings each quarter with additional contributions gleaned from fines levied for breaches of the rules. Non-attendance at a member's funeral for example, "to attend the corpse to the grave in decent apparel" would cost a member a shilling.

The three main items of the actual day of festivities are the church service, the parade and the feast. After an early rise to gather beech branches to decorate *The White Hart* (the historical meeting place of the club) and the church gate, the club members attend the service. There is then a parade through the village with members carrying peeled hazel staves said to represent the staves the Canterbury Pilgrims carried as they passed through the village. Finally we come to the feast; a considerable affair if one is to believe the records. On one such occasion, it is noted that the one hundred club members consumed three 15 lb gammons, 40 lb of veal, 14 lb of topside, 40 lb of salt beef, two legs of pork, six yards of suet pudding and seventy-two gallons of beer. If you manage to coincide your walk with the day of the festivities, I suggest that you lunch early before setting off on your walk or bring some sandwiches with you!

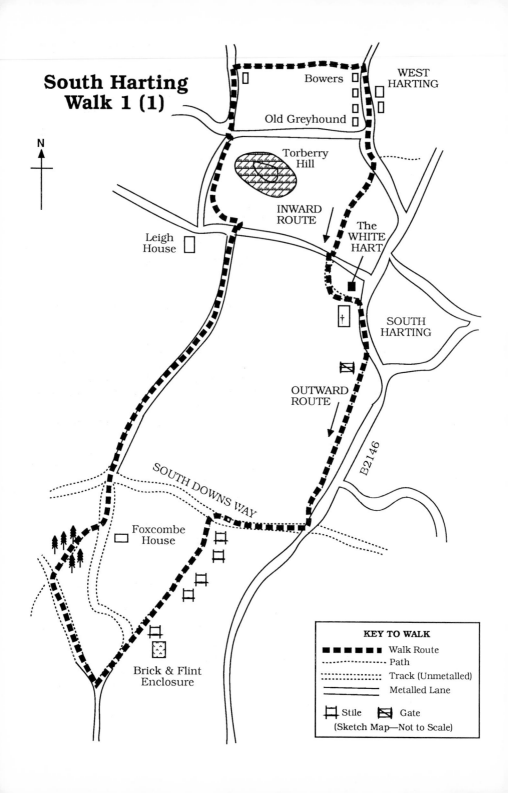

South Harting
Walk 1 (1)

N

WEST HARTING

Bowers

Old Greyhound

Torberry Hill

INWARD ROUTE

Leigh House

The WHITE HART

SOUTH HARTING

OUTWARD ROUTE

B2146

SOUTH DOWNS WAY

Foxcombe House

Brick & Flint Enclosure

KEY TO WALK

▪▪▪▪ Walk Route

·········· Path

:::::::::: Track (Unmetalled)

———— Metalled Lane

⊓ Stile   ⋈ Gate

(Sketch Map—Not to Scale)

South Harting Walk 1

Distance: *Allow 3 hours for this walk, the distance is 6 miles.*

South Harting.

Our walk commences from the centre of South Harting. Walk up through the village with The Church of St. Mary and St. Gabriel on the right. Take very great care here as there is no pavement for a short distance. Just after you pass *The Coach and Horses*, bear off right along the lane that has the pub car park on the left. Walk through the wooden barred gates, continuing along the left side of the grassy public area and then take the footpath up through the woods.

At the top of the hill, turn right and join the South Downs Way. Continue for approximately 700 yards, taking the first footpath off to the left by climbing a stile and cutting across the corner of the field and climbing a further stile to turn left and head south.

This path initially runs through a very narrow section of woodland between the two fields for about 400 yards, until you come to a pair of stiles and enter the small wood. After the wood you then return to walking a narrow strip of woodland, similar to the first section. At the end of this second strip, climb the stile; now take care as it will not be immediately obvious which way to go! Although the way looks overgrown, walk straight on and head to the right hand side of the pond, which is in turn to the right of the brick and flint ruined wall – a sheep pond maybe? Continue along, walking the right side of the field, with a hedgerow of elderberry trees on the right. At the top right corner of this field, you will see a fingerpost. After passing this, swing around to the left and join the bridleway which heads due south.

At the end of the bridleway, at the six-bar metal gate, bear right on to another bridleway which is initially surfaced, but soon turns to shingle as you climb the hill. Where you see the Sussex Border Path (SBP) fingerpost, turn right, joining the SBP and following the earthy path through the pine trees. Emerge from the woods into a clearing, pass a fingerpost sign (vandalised at the time of writing) on your right, and proceed down the hill towards Foxcombe Farm, ahead of you.

At the edge of the wood, take the flinty path past the farm, cross the South Downs Way again and continue down the hill on the SBP. Cross the B2146 by

Leigh House and pick up the 'SBP green fingerpost' almost immediately opposite, walking through the woods leaving the road at a slight angle. The road then runs parallel with the lane – about 20 yards away on the left – to West Harting. After about 600 yards you are obliged to join the lane and at the road junction bear left to head north.

Continue along this lane and leave the SBP at this point by turning right off the road as directed by the fingerpost sign (around the property with the hanging tiles), walking initially with the ditch on your right. Continue following the line of the ditch and then at the next fingerpost sign, turn slightly right across the field. The footpath joins a lane by a small cottage in West Harting called Bowers – turn right here and follow the lane through an attractive collection of timber-framed cottages.

Bear left at the junction by the pink cottage named The Old Greyhound, a one-time pub I believe, following the winding lane to South Harting. Take the footpath off to the right across the field back towards South Harting. Cross the B2146, walking up the narrow lane to the attractive farm buildings. Turn left just in front of these farm buildings and walk between the wooden fences, then bearing left again onto another lane (the drive to the farmhouse), and emerging by South Harting church and the stocks into the main street of the village.

My thanks are due to Mr and Mrs B. Francis who kindly checked this walk for me.

Walk 2

Distance: *Allow 1 hour 40 minutes for this walk, the distance is just over 2 miles.*

Our walk commences from the centre of South Harting. Walk up through the village with The Church of St. Mary and St. Gabriel on the right. Take very great care here as there is no pavement for a short distance. Just after you pass *The Coach and Horses*, bear off right along the lane that has the pub car park on the left.

You then pass into Harting Gardens – a park provided for the enjoyment of Harting residents. Walk along the left side of the grassed area. You then leave this area but keep walking in the same direction up a hill for about 50-100 yards until you come to a junction of footpaths indicated by fingerposts on the left. Carry straight on here past the seat on the right until you come to another junction of footpaths. Then you go straight on until you come to a darker shadier section, through trees. You then meet the road, cross it and join the South Downs Way. This part of the South Downs Way has been surfaced. Your route then descends slowly and you see the B 2141 down on the left. You proceed parallel to this road

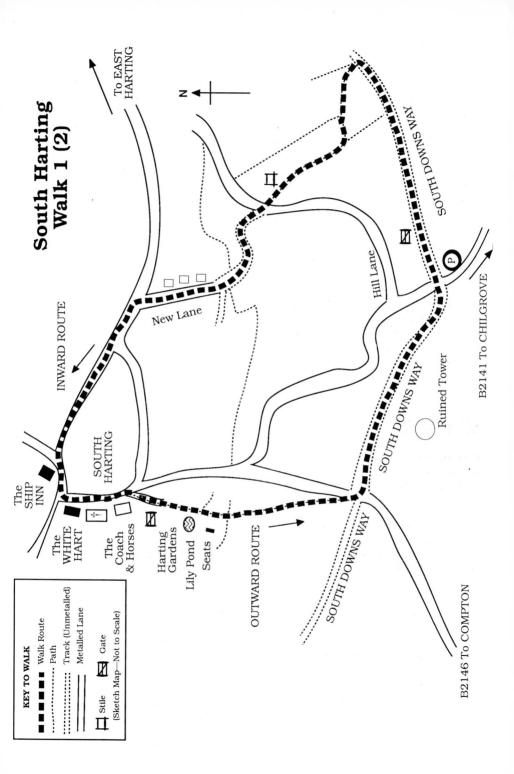

South Harting
Walk 1 (2)

To EAST HARTING

N

SOUTH DOWNS WAY

INWARD ROUTE

New Lane

Hill Lane

P

B2141 To CHILGROVE

SOUTH DOWNS WAY

Ruined Tower

SOUTH DOWNS WAY

The SHIP INN

SOUTH HARTING

The WHITE HART

The Coach & Horses

Harting Gardens

Lily Pond

Seats

OUTWARD ROUTE

SOUTH DOWNS WAY

B2146 To COMPTON

KEY TO WALK

- Walk Route
- Path
- Track (Unmetalled)
- Metalled Lane

Stile   Gate

(Sketch Map—Not to Scale)

for a while and then eventually you cross it to Harting Hill and the car park.

Walk up Harting Hill with the car park on your right. Pass through the small five-bar wooden gate and be careful to close it as requested. Pause here – if time allows – to enjoy the view. If you look to the left a ruined tower can be seen. The origin of the tower is obscure but it would appear that it was built to commemorate the acquisition of land in Virginia USA by members of the Fetherstonhaugh family. The structure fell into a state of disrepair fairly soon after it was constructed. There used to be a story – totally untrue – that the tower was destroyed by angry villagers who believed that wild orgies went on there!

At the top of Harting Hill there is a footpath off to the left which should be ignored. You then start going downhill slightly for the first time in the whole walk. At the next public footpath signpost, bear off left as indicated and head down the hill almost reversing your direction and choosing the route that almost runs parallel with the South Downs Way at first and only gradually descends the hill. The path continues diagonally downhill on a terrace cut into the hillside, that possibly forms part of an ancient earthwork. After about ¼ mile, another path forks off downhill to the right. Ignore this and continue on the main path. At the time of writing there was a fingerpost at this point which had been vandalised. From this point, looking down the hill, it is possible to see two stiles about 200 yards apart, leading into a strip of woodland. We are aiming for the left hand stile. Continue on the terraced path for a short distance until, in open downland, it meets another path at a T-junction, coming from the left from the top of Harting Hill. Turn right here and follow the path down to the stile. Climb this stile – it has a lifting dog hatch – and descend the steps through the trees to the lane below. Take care here as you clamber down the steep bank. Cross over to the track opposite which goes to the left of a partially ornate, iron gate. After bending to the left and then to the right the trackway meets a metalled lane.

Continue straight on down this lane and you soon come to some houses. At the main road turn left taking care as there is no pavement at this point. Follow this road and it takes you back to South Harting village.

My thanks are due to Cliff Barlow who kindly tested this walk for me.

2 · A Short Walk from *The Coach and Horses* at Compton

Background to the Walk

The name "Compton" means a valley farmstead and has been from time to time referred to as Compton St. John to distinguish it from the many other Comptons in the South of England. The "St John" comes not from the local church, but from the Knights of St. John of Jerusalem who owned land here from the 12th to the 14th centuries.

The parish church of St. Mary's Compton is particularly charming and is situated at the end of a little lane close to the starting and finishing point of our walk. There has been a church on this site since pre-Domesday times and like most churches it consists of a mixture of architectural styles. It was last restored in 1849 when it was subject to an extensive programme of alteration, rebuilding and enlargement.

If you are a keen walker of downland areas, you cannot fail to have noticed how frequently the word 'telegraph' occurs on local maps. Telegraph Hill near Winchester for instance, or nearby Telegraph House just south of Beacon Hill. Compton has its own

Map Details
Landranger 1: 50 000
Sheet 197
Pathfinder 1: 25 000
Sheet SU 61/71
Map Reference of
Start/Finish SU786196

Pub Facilities
Food is available at most times. Children are welcome both inside the pub and outside in the garden. There is no objection to dogs. Walkers may park outside, providing the pub is patronised before or after their walk. Please be prepared to take your boots off if you venture into the lounge. Muddy boots are not welcome there, but walkers are! The pub serves some well kept real ales and has a real fire in the winter.

The Coach and Horses, Compton.

How to get there
Compton is situated on the the B 2146 Petersfield to Funtington road about 3 miles south of South Harting. By bus; Compton is served by Southdown Service Nos. 254 and also by Yellowline Tours, both operating from Chichester.

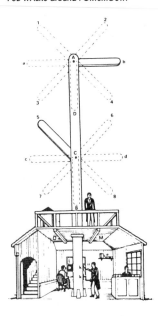

The Semaphore which was used between London and Portsmouth.

Telegraph Hill and it is situated due east of the village.

Although the word 'telegraph' tends to mean electrical signalling these days, during the early part of the last century telegraphy was performed by visual means. A look around the landscape back in those times would have revealed peculiar buildings belonging to, not the post office as you might have imagined, but the Admiralty.

There were two visual signalling methods employed by the Royal Navy between the Admiralty and Portsmouth. The first system was of a temporary nature and was opened in 1796. This was known as the Shutter Telegraph System and consisted of a vertical frame with six sections mounted on top of the station; each section fitted with a shutter that was open or closed.

The Semaphore System was of a more permanent nature and operated from 1822 to 1847. The semaphore arms were 8 feet long, mounted on hexagonal masts 30 feet high.

The station at Compton was part of the semaphore link between Beacon Hill (Telegraph House) and the next station at Portsdown Hill. It was a bungalow type of building and still stands, on the downs above Compton. In his book *The Semaphore*, T.W.Holmes records that the conditions were very severe in the winter. In 1823 the Admiralty Board were told by the lieutenant in charge that 'Man (the Bo'sun signaller hand) is labouring under severe cold in his limbs ... sleeping exposed to weather ... wet drives down the mast, through walls and windows and pavement of the Semaphore room' (in which he had to sling his cot). Not surprisingly, three of the hands became sick with 'severe cold and inflammation of the chest'. Despite these desperate winter conditions, on 2nd January 1832, the station lieutenant had to send an estimate to the Admiralty for a new blanket for his hand. In the Minutes, it is noted that the lieutenant was instructed to obtain one from Lillywhite's (who traded in the village) not exceeding 13/-.

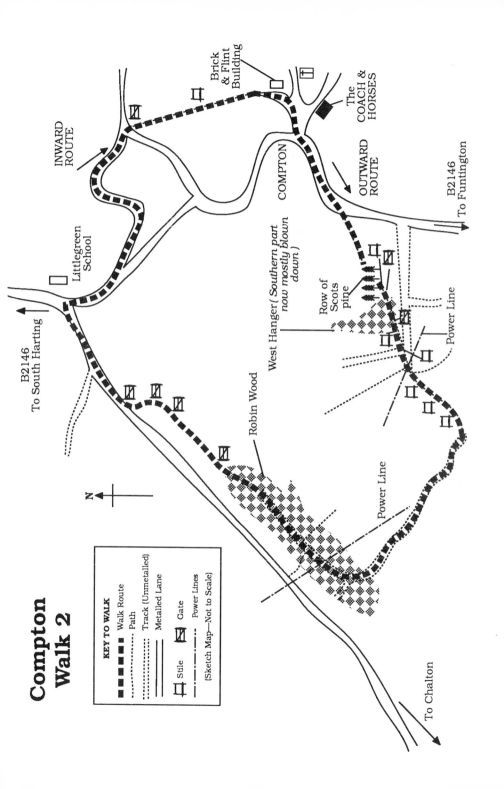

Compton
Walk 2

KEY TO WALK

Walk Route
Path
Track (Unmetalled)
Metalled Lane
Stile
Gate
Power Lines

(Sketch Map—Not to Scale)

INWARD ROUTE

Littlegreen School

B2146 To South Harting

N

OUTWARD ROUTE

COMPTON

Brick & Flint Building

The COACH & HORSES

B2146 To Funtington

West Hanger (*Southern part now mostly blown down*)

Row of Scots pine

Power Line

Robin Wood

Power Line

To Chalton

The Walk

Distance: *Allow 2 hours for this walk, the distance is 4 miles.*

From *The Coach and Horses*, turn left onto the B 2146. After about 250 yards climb the stile on the right (opposite Post Office Cottage) and take the footpath across the field gradually diverging away from the road, aiming for the middle of the Scots pine trees (with their characteristic top heavy appearance) on the opposite side. After a while – how soon depends upon the quality of your eyesight – you will see a stile.

There are actually two stiles here at this strip of woodland. Having climbed both of these, continue in the same direction across the next field until you pass through the stile and gate to enter the remains of storm-damaged West Hanger. Follow the footpath through this short piece of flattened woodland as directed by the fingerpost signs, leaving by the gate and stile into the field.

Walk across this field in a direction slightly to the right of the pylon until you come to the corner of the field where there is a junction of footpaths marked by fingerposts and a small flimsy stile. The footpath that we require heads down a hill under the power lines. You will see a stile, climb over this and there is a fingerpost offering you a choice of two directions. Ignore the footpath that takes you parallel with the fence and take the track that diagonally climbs the hill. At the top of the field you will see a stile. Climb this stile and carry on across this next field toward the top of the hill where you will arrive at another stile in the corner of the field by an oak tree. It is worth pausing here and looking back to enjoy the view of the South Downs with Up Park ahead of you, Compton in the valley below with Telegraph Hill as a backdrop.

Take the trackway marked as a public footpath until after about 150 yards you come to a junction. Bear off to the right here, on the bridleway. Now although this track zig-zags, no directions are needed for about ⅔ mile until you come to the wood (Robin Wood).

At the fingerpost bear right as indicated onto the bridleway through the wood. At the next junction again bear right. After about 30 yards you pass under a power line. Carry on in the same direction ignoring the footpaths off to the left and right.

Eventually when nearly at the edge of the predominantly yew wood follow the direction shown by the bridleway fingerpost sign turning left down the hill. The trackway gradually narrows into a path which eventually delivers you to a five bar metal gate.

Go through the gate and walk along the right hand side of the field and then go through the small five bar gate into the next field. Continue generally in the same direction, roughly parallel to the road on the left, to a small five bar metal gate. Pass through this and after about 30 yards turn left where directed to do so by the fingerpost sign in the field, and walk toward the gate marking access to the road.

Walk down the hill toward Littlegreen, turn right onto the B2146, taking care as there is no pavement and then after about another 300 yards turn left into the narrow lane.

At the junction of lanes (after about ½ mile) turn right and after about 10 yards take the footpath off to the left. Walk in the direction indicated by the fingerpost to the stile at the other side of this large field. Continue in the same direction across the next small field and then follow the track walking past the brick and flint farm building on the left. At the lane, bear right and you are soon back at *The Coach and Horses*.

My thanks are due to Cliff Barlow who kindly tested this walk for me.

Map Details
Landranger 1: 50 000
Sheet 197
Pathfinder 1: 25 000
Sheet SU 60/70
Map Reference of
Start/Finish SU788039

3 · A Walk along the Foreshore from *The Old House at Home*, Chidham

Background to the Walk

For this walk, we forsake the beauty of the downs to encounter a little piece of Holland wedged between Thorney Island and Bosham.

To form a background to this walk, I have tried to discover a little of the history of the parish of Chidham. Every book that I have consulted has told me one thing and one thing only; Chidham is famous for its wheat, known as Chidham White or Hedge Wheat. The reason for the latter name is tied up with the story that you are about to read. It is best told by E.V. Lucas in his *Highways and Byways in Sussex*.

"The wheat was produced more than a century [*now nearly two centuries*] ago by Mr Woods, a farmer. He noticed one afternoon (probably on a Sunday, when farmers are most noticing) an unfamiliar patch of wheat growing in a hedge. It contained

Pub Facilities
Food is available at most times. Children are welcome inside and there is also an outdoor area where they may play. Dogs are welcome as well. Walkers are welcome to park their cars in the car park providing they patronise the pub before or after their walk. The pub serves real ale and has a real fire in the winter months.

How to get there
From Emsworth, take the 'old Chichester road' to Nutbourne. Turn right at the Barleycorn Inn, into Cot Lane and continue onward to The Old House at Home in Chidham.

Old House at Home, Chidham.

24

thirty ears, in which were fourteen hundred corns. Mr Woods carefully saved it and sowed it. The crop was eight pounds and a half. These he sowed, and the crop was forty-eight gallons. Thus it multiplied, until the time came to distribute it to other farmers at a high price". The cultivation of Chidham Wheat at one side of the county, was synchronised with the breeding of Southdown sheep by John Ellman at the other to provide two significant landmarks in agricultural history.

Which way now? Bosham Church from Chidham.

The peninsula of Chidham is a pleasant, quiet and at times windswept sort of place. There is no town or large village and if ever a place could be described as "off the beaten track", this is it. The church of St Mary's somehow fits in perfectly, being not too large or not too small. It is a simple church officially described as being of stone and of Early English style. It dates from 1220 (if one forgets the earlier church on the site) and was restored in 1864.

Looking to the east one sees Bosham. (For the Non-Sussexian visitor there is a quirk of pronunciation to be mastered here. Never rhyme the first syllable with posh. The emphasis should be on the last syllable and pronounced "Bozham"). This view of Bosham and its distinctive church is one of the finest to be had, better even than the approach to Bosham by road. But, the impression gained of Bosham depends on the state of the tide. E.V. Lucas put it very well:

"At high water Bosham is the fair abode of peace. When every straggling arm of the harbour is brimming full, when their still surfaces reflect the sky with a brighter light, and the fishing boats ride erect, Bosham is serenely beautiful and restful. But at low tide she is a slut: the withdrawing floods lay bare vast tracts of mud; the ships heel over into attitudes disreputably oblique; stagnation reigns".

There are many coastal settlements that lay claim to the site of King Canute's realisation of the limits of his royal power. But the inhabitants of Bosham have it, that this is the place where it really happened. He certainly lived here for a while and one of his daughters lies buried in the church. A little later, it was King Harold, the last of the Saxon kings, who set out from Bosham to meet with the

Duke of Normandy which resulted in the Battle of Hastings. Bosham church is featured in the Bayeux Tapestry, where Harold can be seen entering to take sacrament.

To the west of Chidham is Thorney Island. Although the RAF left Thorney in 1976, and the army have since taken their place, it still evokes the feeling that the "boys in light blue" are still there. The airfield, control tower and hangars are visible from the walk and the sailing club is still known, I believe, as the R.A.F. Yachting Club. We have the M.O.D. to thank for this unspoilt view to the west.

Finally we must turn our attention to *The Old House at Home*. A lovely old pub with a lovely old name. It is an appropriate name too; if one ignores the sign and obvious trappings of a pub, it has the air of a well-built, small country house. Beside being unspoilt, it is also a cosy place (after a walk around the foreshore on a cold winter's day), with rain driving against the window and flames leaping up the chimney. It is an interesting pub too, as you will find out if you can get the landlord to tell you about the smuggler's hole that he found, and the old baker's oven in the chimney. Only five years ago Old Chidham Ale was brewed here, in the brewhouse at the back, but the disappearance of this is compensated by the appearance of that legendary brew with the appropriate name – Old Thumper – an ale that seems to produce in me an unfortunate tendency toward double vision.

So while you are warming yourself by the fire, look up and see if you are able to deduce (if sir's mind is not too confused by Old Thumper, or madam's by country wine) the purpose of that agricultural-looking object over the fireplace.

The Walk

Distance: *Allow 2½ hours for this walk, the distance is 5 miles.*

This is a very flat walk that is eminently suitable for the less fit. There is only one stile to negotiate and as there are no sheep, it is very suitable for dogs as well.

From *The Old House at Home*, head northward along the lane. After about 500 yards, turn off left onto the footpath. Walk along the left side of the row of trees, you will have a ditch on your left side. The route meanders while you continue to follow the course of the ditch. As you approach the creek, you will

Chidham
Walk 3

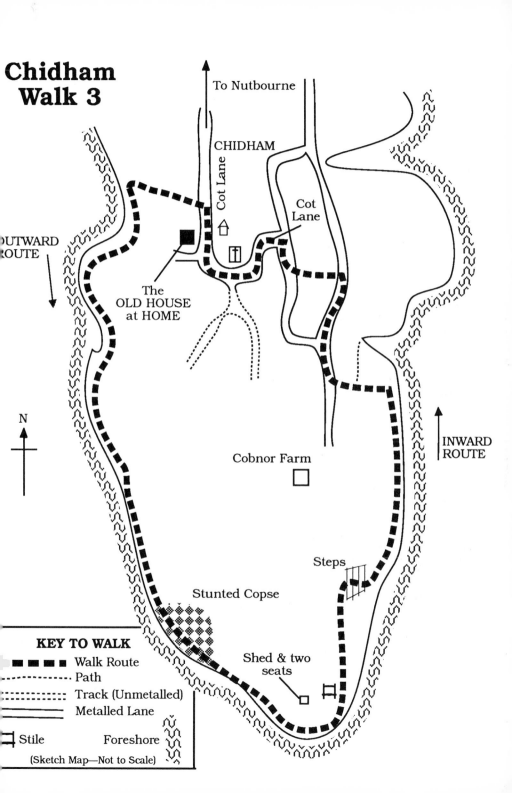

To Nutbourne

CHIDHAM

Cot Lane

Cot
Lane

OUTWARD
ROUTE

The
OLD HOUSE
at HOME

N

Cobnor Farm

INWARD
ROUTE

Steps

Stunted Copse

KEY TO WALK

■ ■ ■ ■ Walk Route

- - - - - - Path

- - - - - - Track (Unmetalled)

———— Metalled Lane

Stile   Foreshore

(Sketch Map—Not to Scale)

Shed & two
seats

have to deviate right slightly to negotiate a ditch before you swing south and walk along the coastal bank.

Very few directions are required now, until you are nearly upon the small wood. Here you will need to walk along the foreshore instead of the raised bank. There are interesting exposed oak tree roots here. The next landmark is the pair of seats by the shed. This is a handy place to stop for refreshment as it is approximately the half-way point.

Continue along the foreshore, negotiate the stile and then climb onto the raised bank. The route then swings northward on a rather pleasant shingly path that has been specially built for disabled people. It is soon necessary to divert inland for a short distance as it is not possible to continue along the shore. Walk through the boat mooring area and at the end of the gravelly footpath, walk across the grass toward the fingerpost sign, continue onward in the direction indicated, crossing the small footbridge. Cross the gravel track, proceed down the right hand side of the next field and around the right side of the pond. Bear right, climb the steps and you will be back again on the coast.

After about 600 yards swing inland and follow the fingerposted footpath, avoiding the footpath that continues along the creek, until you reach the lane where you turn right for a short distance until the T Junction. Here you turn right and follow the lane toward Chidham. The road bears sharply to the left; at this point take the footpath to the left past the telephone box – a good old-fashioned red type! This is a pleasant grassy path, continue until you reach the lane, where you turn right.

Pass 'The White Cottage' on the right and then proceed along Cot Lane past the church also on the right and in no time at all you will be back at your starting point.

My thanks are due to Roger and Gillian Riley who kindly tested this walk for me.

4 · An Ascent of Beacon Hill from *The Shoe* at Exton

Background to the Walk

"Exton" seems to be a Saxon word meaning "East Saxons Farm". The pub name *The Shoe* is what is known as a "calling" sign, that is it refers to a trade or calling. Whether this is the case here or not, the pub sign depicting an old-fashioned, buckled shoe is a colourful one. This thirties-style pub, built on the site of an earlier hostelry, is not a particularly attractive building; it is its situation close to the sparkling River Meon that makes it a pub worthy of note. On a warm mid-summer evening after a long walk, buy your refreshments, cross the road, open the little garden gate and relax. There is nothing quite so soothing as watching and listening to water trickling and gurgling past in its unhurried way. The many ducks, mostly mallard, are a constant source of amusement for the younger members of the family, practicing their take-offs and landings and squabbling from time to time over a soggy crisp. In addition to the ducks, you may very well see a Heron

Maps
Landranger 1: 50 000 Sheet 185
Pathfinder 1: 25 000 Sheet SU 42/52 and SU 62/72
Map Reference of Start/Finish SU613208

Pub Facilities
Meals are available at most times. There is a delightful riverside garden where children may feed the ducks. Dogs are permitted in at least one area of the pub. The pub has only a small car park so it is recommended that you park where shown on the sketch map. Real ale is served and the pub has a real fire.

Alternative Facilities
The George and Falcon at Warnford is also a very popular pub.

The Shoe at Exton.

How to get there
The walk starts from Exton. Park your car at Point (P) on the sketch map, ensuring that it is locked securely and with any items of value removed as thefts from cars have occurred in this area. The walk is written assuming a start at this point. Exton and Warnford are served by the Southampton Citybus Service No. 52/52A from Petersfield to Southampton.

ghosting by slowly overhead following the course of the Meon. And, if your feet are hot and tired, then why not indulge in the ultimate luxury of plunging them in the constantly cool waters of the River Meon.

In many respects the Sussex countryside has the edge over Hampshire's, but this is not true of its rivers. The rivers of Sussex are sluggish, brackish and unhealthy looking, while the Itchen, Test and Meon are true crystal clear chalk streams where trout swim lazily among the green weeds. The water from the downland springs, issues forth at an almost constant temperature changing little through the year. These streams are greatly affected by the calcium that they carry, leading for instance to many water-snails that need the calcium to build their shells. It is not uncommon for these streams to be widened and modified to form watercress beds – there are some immediately upstream at Warnford and these are excellent places to watch birds.

The words Itchen and Meon are very old. The Meonwara were early English invaders that took their name from this river. They lived a secluded life on farms, largely isolated from outside influences by the surrounding high downland of Beacon Hill and Old Wincester Hill. They were untouched by Christianity until the seventh century when Wilfred Archbishop of York worked as a missionary among them.

Old writers of the countryside of Victorian and Edwardian times, were fond of identifying racial differences in the people of different localities. One such writer describes the men (he omits to mention the women) of the Meon Valley as "tall dark and intelligent, they stand apart and are often said to preserve the Jutish type, the long skull and face and nose and the big chin".

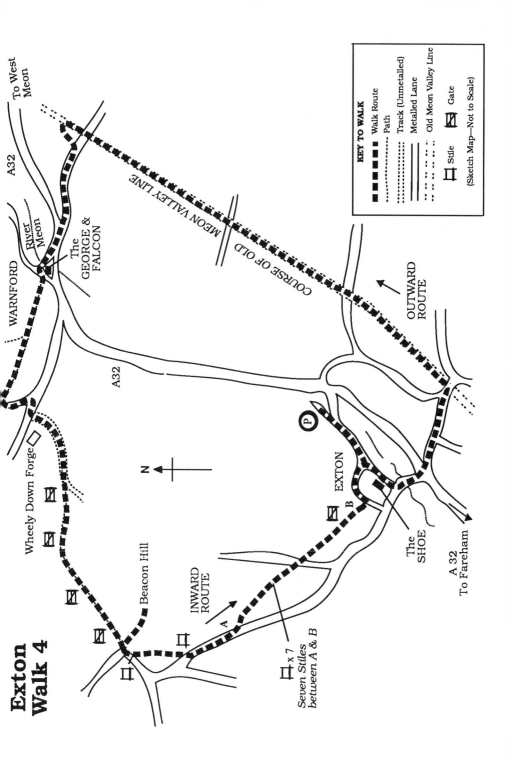

Exton
Walk 4

KEY TO WALK

Walk Route
Path
Track (Unmetalled)
Metalled Lane
Old Meon Valley Line

Stile   Gate

(Sketch Map—Not to Scale)

To West Meon

A32

River Meon

WARNFORD

The GEORGE & FALCON

MEON VALLEY LINE

COURSE OF OLD

OUTWARD ROUTE

A32

Wheely Down Forge

N

Beacon Hill

INWARD ROUTE

A

EXTON

B

The SHOE

A 32 To Fareham

x 7
Seven Stiles between A & B

The Walk

Distance: This is a longish walk (7¾ miles) and will take you up to 4 hours. During mid-winter you will need to set off before lunch to finish the walk before nightfall.

The Punch Bowl near Beacon Hill.

The final leg of the walk from the point (A) on the map to (B) is a very steep descent of Beacon Hill and (at the time of writing) crosses a field of wet cabbages, with the right of way particlarly badly marked. If you wish, you can take a pleasant country lane instead, as shown on the map.

From the point marked (P) on the sketch map, by the entrance to Manor Farm, walk toward Exton Village. Turn left at the junction of roads, by the cream and green house. Follow the road through the village and past *The Shoe* until you are at the main A32.

Carefully cross and take the lane that is almost opposite and climb the steep hill. Continue on this lane – avoiding the left turn marked No Through Road. Pass through the remains of the demolished railway arch and immediately turn left using the gravel path to climb to the top of the old railway embankment.

Little direction is required here, just follow the route of the old Meon Valley Line in a north-easterly direction (descending the route just once to cross a lane) until you pass under the high arch. Here; walk on for about 200 yards, and then turn sharp left, almost reversing in direction, to climb the gravel track, back up to the road (ignore the stile on the right).

Turn right when you reach the road until you arrive at Warnford. Take the lane that runs to the right of *The George and Falcon* car park, cross the River

Meon and turn left. The white building on your right is the Meon Valley Study Centre. At the end of this building turn right, and follow the public footpath up the hill that runs on the gravel track and concrete drive.

At the top of the hill, you will see a fingerpost indicating two footpaths. Take the left-most route, walking toward the right hand corner of the small copse ahead of you. (The landowner has been known to plough the field without restoring the footpath). There is also a so-called courtesy path that runs around the edge of the field – use it if you wish. By the copse, continue on the trackway that runs between the two fields. By the solitary tree turn left – there should be a yellow arrow indicating your way.

Walk with a hedgerow on your right that contains a mixture of brambles and elderberry. Ignore the stile in the hedgerow. At the end of the field you meet a crossing trackway. Turn left and descend the hill on this gravel trackway that runs between hedgerows. When you meet the road turn right and after about 200 yards turn left on the gravel track by Wheely Down Forge.

Our route follows this track for about another 200 yards or so, and then our way turns right, off the track, through the gate/stile; turn left initially walking parallel with the fence, and then following the line of the 'guide-posts'. On this beautiful stretch of rolling downland you pass through three gates before you reach the wood. Continue through the wood until you reach the road (on it's bend). I would strongly advise a detour here to enjoy the views from Beacon Hill. You can see the Solent, Isle of Wight, Old Winchester Hill, Butser Hill and much more. Turn left here then if you wish and follow the track to the viewpoint.

From Beacon Hill, re-trace your steps until you almost reach the road again and turn left over the rickety stile, and take a line diagonally across the field toward the solitary tree in the hedgerow on the other side of this field. About 60 yards further along, (to the left) you will find the stile which you climb to enter the road.

Turn left on this road and after about 400 yards take the footpath to the left at (A), or keep to the road if you wish. Assuming you have taken the path, take a line gradually away from the road, aiming for the narrow stile between the gap in the beech trees. The next stile (or more correctly pair of stiles) is in the bottom corner of the field. Cross the next field, climb the stile and cross a further field. The stile at the edge of this field marks a junction with a trackway. Cross it and continue through this field (that had the very wet cabbages). Take the stile into the next field and after about 250 yards turn left, following the line of the hedgerow passing through the gate (probably open) down to the road (B) where you turn left and return to the start of the walk.

My thanks are due to Mr and Mrs B. Francis who kindly tested this walk for me.

Map Details
Landranger 1: 50 000
Sheet 197
Pathfinder 1: 25 000
Sheet SU 60/70 (1304)
Map Reference of
Start/Finish SU759057

5 · Follow the Sussex Border Path from Hermitage near Emsworth

Pub Facilities

The Sussex Brewery.
Food is available at most times and there is a room where children are permitted. There is also an outdoor garden. Dogs are allowed in the pub. Walkers are welcome to park their cars in the pub car park, providing they patronise the pub before or after their walk. The car park is not over-large and at busy times it might be best to park in Emsworth while walking – shown (P) on sketch map. The pub has real ale and real fires in winter.

How to get there

From Portsmouth, take the Emsworth Exit from the A27 and then follow the A259 to the Emsworth roundabout.
Emsworth can be reached by bus and train from Havant, Portsmouth and Chichester.

Refreshment Facilities

Aside from The Sussex Brewery, Emsworth has the grand total of 12 public houses where you can refresh yourself and also Heidi's coffee house in the town centre.

Background to the Walk

The Sussex Brewery is one of the few remaining ale-houses in Sussex where ale is still brewed. It is a charming old pub, full of characters, with two small connected bars whose floors are sprinkled with sawdust.

The brewery is in a creeper-covered building at the side of the pub. It can be confirmed that ale was brewed on this site at least as far back as 1869 at which time there were three small local breweries. The owner believes that brewing on the site goes back considerably further to 500 years ago when it was known as the Saffron Brewery. However, brewing ceased in the late 19th century and the pub closed its doors in the 1960's. The resurgence of real ale, led a dedicated band of enthusiasts to spend four years in the late 1970's on restoring the derelict pub. It was opened again in 1979 to be followed by

Sussex Brewery.

the opening of a full-mash brewery in 1981. I believe that three ales are now brewed there: Wyndham's Bitter, Hermitage Best Bitter and Warrior Ale, and that almost all of the production goes to the pub itself. To be able to visit a pub such as this and taste the locally brewed ale is one of the simplest and best pleasures of life. How thankful we should be that CAMRA has managed to reverse the trend towards "bigger breweries brewing blander beer".

If you want to know the very interesting history of Emsworth, then you should read Mr David Rudkin's excellent series of books that contain all that is worth knowing of the Emsworth area. I am indebted to him for all of the following information and also much oral history that he has conveyed to me.

Emsworth gains its name from the watercourse that rises in Stoughton, and flows via Racton and Westbourne and thence via a number of routes to Emsworth Harbour. Over the course of time since the 12th Century, the village has been known by several names. The earliest name for the town now known as Emsworth was Neutebrigge, which is thought to mean causeway or bridge not belonging to either the Hampshire or Sussex side of the Ems. Next appears Emelsworth or Emilsworth and Emmesworth and Empnesworth are later variants. 'Ems', is of course, the name of the river and 'worth' means a protected settlement – that is, a town with some sort of defence around it. Linking the two together simply gives us the town on the River Ems.

Although our walk does not take us to the harbour, it is only a short distance away and I would like to dwell for a moment or two on the most prominent features of Emsworth's maritime past.

If Emsworth has been famous for anything, it is oysters and scallops. The towns oysters have been justifiably sought after over the years; there was a sizeable oyster fleet at the turn of the century. However, in 1902 the town became not only famous for its oysters but also infamous! In the closing months of that year, many people were taken ill (some subsequently died) with Typhoid Fever, after feasting at corporation banquets in Winchester and Southampton. After investigation, Emsworth oysters, served as a starter course, were identified as the cause.

At that time, untreated sewage was discharged into the harbour very close to the oyster beds, causing contamination. Oysters from Emsworth were, as you would expect, not the most sought after food product for quite a while, until the building of a new sewage treatment works in 1914. Needless to say there was lengthy litigation between the council and an oyster bed owner.

Smuggling in south coast maritime towns was common in the past and Emsworth was no exception, with wine, spirits and tobacco being brought in from the continent, often via Thorney Island.

Emsworth also felt the hand of the press gangs from Portsmouth Dockyard. There is a story that one of the gangs visited John King's shipyard to obtain the services of some of his men. Mr King shut the shipyard's iron gates and threatened to cut off the hand of anyone that opened them. He fed the men for several days while a rider was dispatched to the yard to seek exemption for the men, who were engaged on naval contracts.

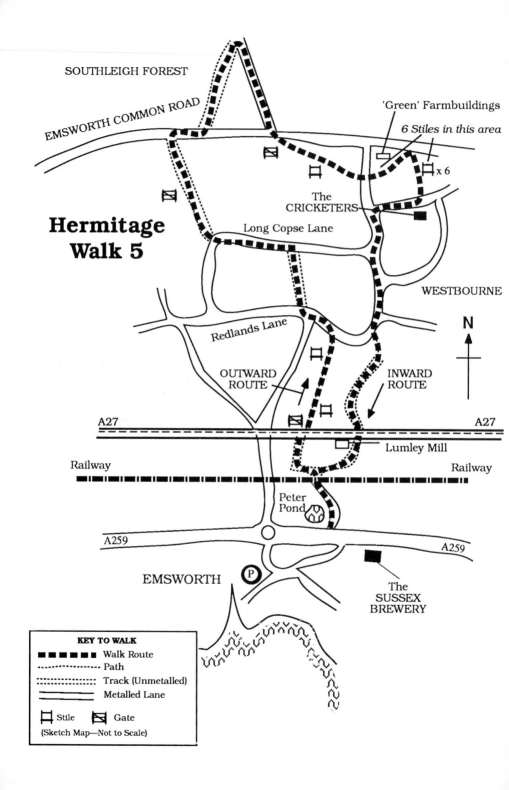

SOUTHLEIGH FOREST

EMSWORTH COMMON ROAD

'Green' Farmbuildings

6 Stiles in this area

x 6

The
CRICKETERS

Hermitage
Walk 5

Long Copse Lane

WESTBOURNE

N

Redlands Lane

OUTWARD
ROUTE

INWARD
ROUTE

A27   A27

Lumley Mill

Railway   Railway

Peter
Pond

A259   A259

EMSWORTH

P

The
SUSSEX
BREWERY

KEY TO WALK

■ ■ ■ ■ ■ Walk Route

. . . . Path

: : : : : : : : : : : : : Track (Unmetalled)

———————— Metalled Lane

Stile   Gate

(Sketch Map—Not to Scale)

PUB WALKS around PORTSMOUTH

The Walk

Distance: *Allow 3 hours for this walk, the distance is 5¾ miles.*

As *The Sussex Brewery*'s car park is not over-large I have written the directions for this walk from Emsworth Town Centre, in case you park there. If you start from *The Sussex Brewery*, just pick up Lumley Road on the other side of the A259.

From South Street, turn right by *The Smugglers* and follow the road around into Queen Street, passing *The Lord Raglan* on the right. Cross the A259 and walk along Lumley Road on the right side of the pond. This is the upper reach of the millpond that fed the old Slipper Mill. The pond was tidal, replenished at high tide by the sea and to a lesser extent by the Ems. It was reputedly the last tidal mill to have been operational, eventually ceasing work in 1940.

After a while you will walk parallel with the watercourse. At the end of the lane (by Lumley Mill) turn left as indicated by the public footpath sign. The path we are following is marked "Sussex Border Path 1989".

Walk along the enclosed path. At its end, turn right through the concrete posts and walk along the gravel track that takes you underneath the A27 dual carriageway. Pass through the small wooden gate and head toward the wartime 'pillbox' in the distance. Walk for about 70 yards on an enclosed path, climb the stile and then walk generally along the left side following the fairly well-worn line of the path. At the end of the field it is easy to miss your exit. It is important to look for the stile on the left – it can be partially hidden by the hedge. Walk the narrow enclosed path to the road.

Turn left onto Westbourne Road. At the mini-roundabout, turn right into Redlands Lane and where the lane bears to the left, take the path off to the right that passes through the concrete posts. Follow this path until it meets Long Copse Lane where you turn left. By the entrance to Hollybank House, turn right onto the track.

Before long you will pass through a six-bar metal gate, with a stile alongside, continue along the track in a generally northerly direction – you will eventually meet the very busy Emsworth Common Road where you turn right and follow it for approximately 400 yards until you see a (usually boggy) bridleway off to the left through the woods. Follow the path through the woods until you meet the next lane (Woodberry Lane), turn right.

When you meet Emsworth Common Road again, cross straight over through the rusty metal gate into the field, climbing one stile before you meet the next lane. Cross this into the next field, by climbing the next stile and aiming yourself toward the right side of the green farm buildings. Climb the strongly constructed stile, pass around the farm and you will see two stiles. Now the correct route (but a bit of a dog's leg) is to use the left one, proceed towards the road, turn sharp right and come back to the other stile – I leave it to you to choose your route to the right hand stile.

Continue towards Westbourne climbing three stiles in a straight line until you arrive at *The Cricketers*. Here turn right into Silverlock Place which in turn leads into North Street. Follow North Street through Westbourne. At the road junction turn right, passing *The White Horse Inn* on the left.

Opposite the church, turn left and follow the path that follows the watercourse. When you approach the A27, Mill Lane deviates from its original course to meet the new bridge. Follow Mill Lane as far as Lumley Millhouse.

Lumley Mill complete with peep holes to keep an eye on the workers.

Lumley Mill has an interesting story. It was purchased in 1806 by Mr Edward Tollervey, who became very rich, earning his fortune supplying the Royal Navy with provisions. He made major enhancements to the property adding a store, piggery and bakehouse – he hoped to corner the naval provision market.

Hard times ensued and an extravagant lifestyle led to his bankruptcy. In 1830 he was placed in Westbourne Poor House (the site of which we passed earlier on the walk, on the corner of Covington Road), but his downfall was too much to bear with dignity, and the records of the Poor House proved that he became an upsetting influence on the old, young and sick inhabitants of the Poor House and he was asked to leave. The sad story of Mr Tollervey continues in London where he was later seen by an old acquaintance in the guise of a crossing sweeper. He asked for charity from his friend and was given a new broom and barrow, in response to his request. He is thought to have passed away shortly after this!

The attractive flint houses by the mill house were built by Mr Tollervey to house his mill wagons and were part of his general improvements.

The actual mill building was destroyed by fire in 1915 but the remaining mill house is an extremely attractive building. The small oval peepholes in the oval recesses were apparently inserted to enable Mr Tollervey to watch his employees at work without being seen himself.

After Lumley Mill no further directions are necessary for your return to Emsworth, as you have now rejoined your original route.

My thanks are due to Bert and Pat Morrisey who kindly tested this walk.

6 · Two Walks from *The George Inn* at Finchdean

Maps
Landranger 1: 50 000
Sheet 197
Pathfinder 1: 25 000
Sheet SU 61/71
Map Reference of
Start/Finish SU739127

Background to the Walks

If you were to draw a straight line on a map from Petersfield to Havant, it would pass through Finchdean. This lovely village is surrounded on all sides by gentle chalk hills. The largest of these is Idsworth Down to the north, with Wick Hanger to the west and a gentler slope to the east, apparently not of sufficient importance to warrant a name.

Although it is an attractive settlement, it is not what one would call a picture postcard village; there are no large or grand houses, few thatched dwellings that I can recollect and there is, quite rightly, just a little industry – not the huge aluminium clad boxes that proliferate these days, but buildings of a more human scale.

There was until recently at the north end of the village, the Finchdean Ironworks. This has now been skilfully converted into housing in a most agreeable way. One product of the ironworks can be seen in the row of cottages built for the Ironworks employees

Pub Facilities
Food is available at most times at The George. Children are welcome in the Restaurant only and there is a large field and garden in which children may play. Dogs are permitted in the bar. Please park your car in the spaces by the village green as the pub car park is small. There is a good selection of real ale from the Ind Coope range, open fires in the winter and a payphone is available.

How to get there
Assuming travel from Portsmouth or the north, via the A3M, take the Horndean/Emsworth Exit. Cross over the motorway following the directions to Horndean and Emsworth. Take the next left (B2149) toward Horndean and next right (signposted Finchdean 2½ miles). From this point just follow the directions to Finchdean, and park near the village green, by the blacksmith's forge.

Finchdean Ironworks – now converted into houses.

Don't forget your pub stamp.

Additional Facilities
In addition to The George Inn at Finchdean there are three pubs to choose from in Rowlands Castle. There is also an excellent cafe – The Coffee Pot – that sells the most delicious home-made cakes.

by their benevolent employer (John Cannings) in neighbouring Dean Lane End – the unusual iron windows were made in the ironworks. On the small village green there is a forge that is still used as an active smithy, with a tyring plate outside used to hold a wagon wheel, while the steel tyre is fitted.

At the centre of things, sitting in a perfect position to keep a watchful eye on the village green and everything that passes through the village is *The George Inn.*

I am not sure of the age of the current building, but the proceedings of the Finchdean Hundred records the sale of "all that cottage or dwellinghouse, brewhouse, stable, garden, orchard and all the other outhouses, with about one acre of ground, part of the mast of the said manor of Idsworth" in 1783 with an indication that it originally existed as far back as 1740. This sale was to a William Marshall who also owned some land in the vicinity of the green known as Marshall's Piece. It would appear that Marshall, who was probably a blacksmith, bought the inn for the accommodation of riders of horses waiting for shoeing and as a resting place for weary travellers.

Perhaps the most interesting aspect of *The George Inn* is that every spring there is celebrated here, the ancient festival of Hocktide. It was staged in the Finchdean Hundred up until 1651 and revived a few years ago by Norman Green to whom I am indebted for this history. Although for practical reasons it is now held on the May Day Bank Holiday Monday, originally it was held on the second Monday and Tuesday after Easter.

It was a festival that marked the end of winter and the coming of spring. The village was decorated, bounds were walked to establish land ownership and various forest rights, and hocked animals were released from their winter quarters to enjoy the freedom of the new grass, which probably gave the festival its name.

On Hock Monday, the women siezed and bound men on the public roads with ropes, demanding a token payment for their release; on Hock Tuesday the roles were reversed and it was the men's turn.

Another charming feature was that the local men met to give Frankpledge – sometimes known as

Frithborth – where they promised good behaviour and helpful ways and gave a public account of their behaviour.

Not all of these activities are undertaken now, but the spirit of the event is I believe, still the same, with emphasis on village crafts and pastimes. You can rest assured that even if you visit the village at Hocktide you are not likely to be kidnapped or forced to give a public account of your behaviour, but you will, no doubt, find plenty of scope for walking the bounds.

Some villages have virtually no footpaths and some have many. Finchdean falls into the latter category enabling the preparation of two walks for this book. Apart from the four vehicular rights of way there are six or so "green ways" of entering the village. The Sussex Border Path – a lesser long distance route – also passes through the village centre. These routes provide tens of miles of footpath waiting to be explored in almost complete solitude at most times of the year.

The two walks that follow are of medium length of about 5½ miles. Try to find time to visit *The George* – it is a pub full of local worthies who have not heard of upward mobility! If you like strong ale, you will find the Burton Ale is unsurpassed for quality, being very well kept (a few degrees cooler than normal), making it the most refreshing of drinks for summer months. May the world never change!

The George Inn at Finchdean.

Walk 1

Distance: *Allow 2 ¾ hours for this walk, the distance is 5½ miles.*

The little church in the field.

Waterproof footwear should be considered, as the track that passes Horsley Farm is usually waterlogged in wet weather.

From the village green, take the country road signposted to Chalton (with the old smithy on your right). After a short distance you will come to a footpath fingerpost sign on your right – by the end of Ashcroft Lane. Take this footpath by climbing the stile and walking parallel with the road until you reach the boundary edge of the field. Turn right and start climbing the hill.

At first, a hedgerow accompanies you on the left for most of the way as you gradually climb Idsworth Down.

You cross an open section of field for a short distance and are then joined by a copse on the left. A disused stile will appear with yellow arrows confirming your way. At the next disused stile there is also a fingerpost sign: here you turn left for roughly 200 yards and then bear right by the old tree stump. Continue your walk with conifers and some old yews on your left and after a short distance you will meet a bridleway crossing the path. Turn right at this point, following the route that winds down towards Heberdens.

Cross the railway line very carefully, close the gates and do not loiter. Cross the road and walk up towards St Huberts Church (taking the footbridge if the Lavants are up). Often known as the "Little Church in the Field", its beauty lies in its simplicity. It was originally dedicated to St Peter and St Paul in 1053, and is named after the patron saint of hunters. Within, on the north wall of the chancel, are notable wall paintings that date from around 1300 and depict scenes of St Hubert and John the Baptist.

The route skirts around the left side of the church. Climb the stile and then turn immediately left (following the signed diversion) in the direction of the road and then walk parallel with the road for about 130 yards. Climb the stile and

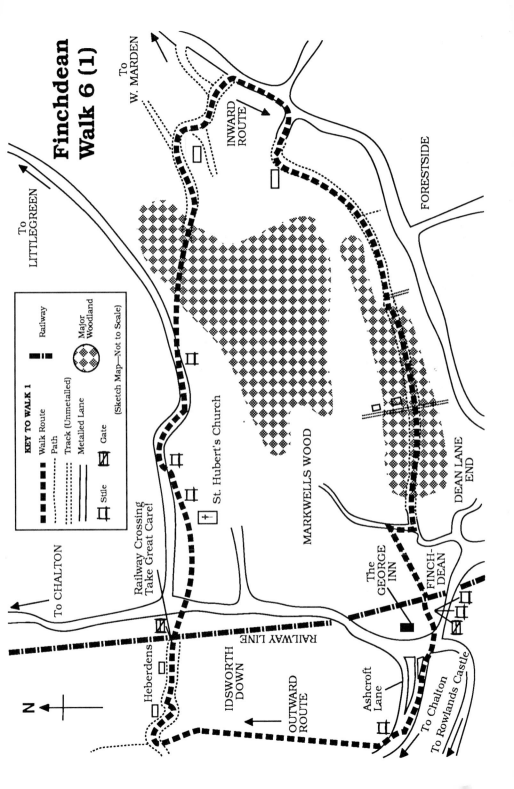

Finchdean
Walk 6 (1)

KEY TO WALK 1

Walk Route
Path
Track (Unmetalled)
Metalled Lane
Railway
Major Woodland

Stile
Gate

(Sketch Map—Not to Scale)

To LITTLEGREEN

To W. MARDEN

INWARD ROUTE

FORESTSIDE

MARKWELLS WOOD

St. Hubert's Church

Railway Crossing Take Great Care!

To CHALTON

Heberdens

IDSWORTH DOWN

OUTWARD ROUTE

RAILWAY LINE

The GEORGE INN

FINCH-DEAN

DEAN LANE END

Ashcroft Lane

To Chalton

To Rowlands Castle

N

turn right, following the Littlegreen road for about 600 yards.

Leave the road just after the S bend, following the footpath to the right that crosses a narrow strip of ploughed field toward a dual fingerpost sign. Walk diagonally up the hill. Climb the the steep bank and turn left up the hill as directed by the fingerpost sign. Be careful here as you could miss the exit from this track! After roughly 150 yards leave the trackway by climbing up the bank on your right (the point is marked by a fingerpost sign) to follow a narrower route that initially proceeds between fir trees. After a steepish climb, you will reach the edge of the wood (open field on your right); pass between two rustic wooden barriers and walk a further 20 yards or so until you are by a fingerpost sign. Proceed straight on at this point and leave the wood.

Follow a boggy bridleway and at the three-way junction bear right. When you are at Horsley Farm, proceed straight on, continuing to follow the bridleway. Ignore the bridleway off to the left (to West Marden) and proceed straight on along the lane until you come to the road, where you turn right.

Follow the road for about 400 yards and then turn off right into a lane. This lane is metalled for a short distance and then becomes a track. When you arrive at the edge of Shortleys Copse avoid the left turn into the field and carry straight on down the hill.

You will come to a clearing – there is the remains of a very old, timber-framed house on your right – proceed straight on through some delightful coppiced woodland until you eventually come to a skewed cross-roads.

Bear right onto the metalled lane and after about 300 yards take the footpath on the left. Walk under the small railway arch, over the stile, along the path between the fences, over a further stile and take your exit from the field via the very wide gate, and proceed back to the green.

My thanks are due to Peter Holloway who kindly tested this walk for me.

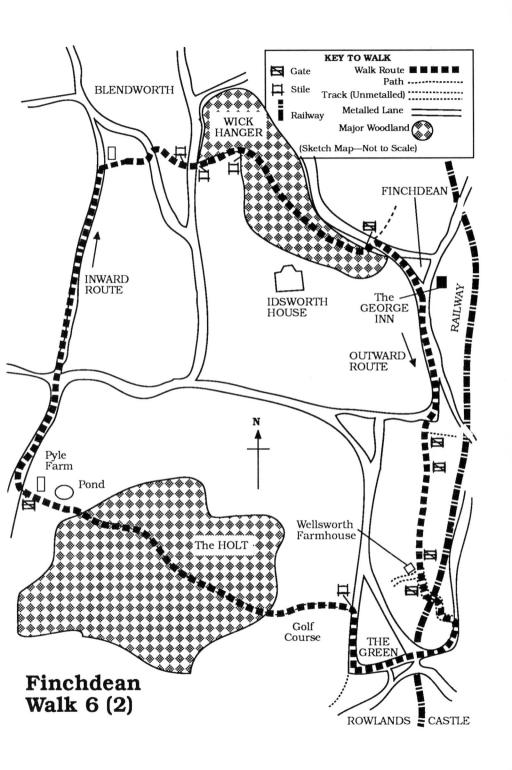

KEY TO WALK

Gate

Stile

Railway

Walk Route

Path

Track (Unmetalled)

Metalled Lane

Major Woodland

(Sketch Map—Not to Scale)

BLENDWORTH

WICK HANGER

FINCHDEAN

INWARD ROUTE

IDSWORTH HOUSE

The GEORGE INN

RAILWAY

OUTWARD ROUTE

N

Pyle Farm

Pond

The HOLT

Wellsworth Farmhouse

Golf Course

THE GREEN

Finchdean
Walk 6 (2)

ROWLANDS CASTLE

Walk 2

Distance: *The total distance of the walk is 5½ miles. Allow 2 ¾ hours.*

From the green, take the Rowlands Castle road, passing *The George Inn*, forking right after approximately 60 yards and climbing the hill (known as White Hill). Where the road bends sharply to the right, almost at the top of the hill, take the footpath off to the left (your visibility of oncoming traffic will be better if you cross to the left side of the road before you get to the bend).

You will see a footpath on the left – ignore this – and walk around the right side of the metal bar gate and then around a further similar gate. After a third gate, bear left at Wellsworth Farmhouse and left at the fork and continue on until you reach the gate/stile. Here you bear right and follow the path to the railway bridge. Walk over the bridge and follow the gravelly path down to the road, where you turn right, and use the road to walk into Rowlands Castle.

Walk past the green (on your left) and follow Links Lane. Pass the golf club-house (also on your left) and continue on for about 600 yards. Take the footpath off to the left just after Holt Gardens. Climb the stile and follow the gravelly track until the point where it meets the concrete drive. Here bear left and cross the golf course aiming for the row of small hawthorn trees – walk with them on your right and enter the wood. Although you have right of way across the course, please display courtesy towards the golfers and minimise interruption to play.

Enter the quiet wood (The Holt) and follow the path (crossing one metalled track) until you arrive at the woodland edge. Climb the stile and walk through the field following the line of the two trees. Walk with the pond on your right, continuing toward the five-bar wooden gate marking the exit to the road.

Turn right and walk along the lane, passing Pyle Farm. At the cross-roads, carry straight on (but take very great care as it is difficult to see approaching traffic from the right). After about half a mile take the footpath off to the right, by the brick and flint cottage. Take the path along the left side of the field. At the end of the field join the lane, turn left and where the hedgerow on the right ends, take the footpath off to the right, and again walk along the left side of the field (alongside the thick hedgerow).

Use the stiles to cross the road, continue walking until you climb a further stile and enter the wood (Wick Hanger). Walk for 20 yards and turn right at the fingerpost sign. You will cross a crossing track and be joined by a fence on your right. At the end of the fence bear left and follow the track which after 20 yards bends to the right and then proceeds down through Wick Hanger to the road. Turn right at the road and walk through Finchdean back to the green.

My thanks are due to Peter Holloway who kindly tested this walk for me.

7 · A Riverside Walk from *The Black Horse* at Byworth

Background to the Walk

Byworth's name is an appropriate one. Although the village is within a stone's throw of the A283 – the busy Petworth to Pulborough road – it lies alongside a little lane which is very much a byway.

Do not be put off by your initial external impression of *The Black Horse*. It is a three-storey, tall, thin and rather gaunt looking building that would perhaps look more at home as a small London hotel rather than a country pub.

The front door, however, has the homely look of a normal domestic front door, which encourages you within. As soon as you enter you will find that that this pub, like all good pubs, is simply furnished. Stripped pews, scrubbed tables and bare floorboards. It is a pub with a wide range of good food, although you will not feel out of place merely enjoying a drink there. The general age of the building lends much atmosphere to the interior, because although the front of the building was built around 1821, the main rear part dates from the 16th century and is thought to have been a friary. The garden is terraced and drops down to a large lawn at the bottom beside a stream and old willow tree. An interesting feature is that the pub has an old sign at the rear of the building, alongside the field footpath; a relic no doubt of when local dwellers walked to *The Black Horse* rather than using their cars – a feature to which we seem to be returning

My final reason for liking *The Black Horse* was that at the time of my visit there – a few days before Christmas – they were only just putting up their Christmas decorations. How refreshing it is to find a business that is not a slave to the modern trend of starting the festival of Christmas in early autumn.

Any walk around the Petworth area has to be on the south side of the town. There are few public

Maps
Landranger 1: 50 000
Sheet 197
Pathfinder 1: 25 000
Sheet SU 82/92
Map Reference of
Start/Finish SU987211

Pub Facilities
Food is available at most times. Children are welcome if well behaved. There is an outdoor garden where children may sit. Dogs are permitted if on a lead but very large dogs are not encouraged. Walkers are welcome to park their cars in the pub car park providing they patronise the pub before or after their walk, but prior notice of 12 or more persons would be appreciated. The pub has a payphone available for customers use. Real ale is served and there is a real fire in the winter months.

How to get there
Byworth is situated just off the A283 – take the first right coming out of Petworth.

47

Pub facade built around 1821.

footpaths toward the north and the west is shut off with no public rights of way over several square miles due to the enclosed land of Petworth Park. What a scandalous situation it is, that the people of this nation do not have open access to land which is allegedly held in trust for them.

Our walk takes us through Petworth and alongside the slow-moving River Rother (the west one, for there are two) and enables us to enjoy views of the South Downs in the distance. Petworth is a feudal town, similar in nature to Arundel. It is totally dominated by the Petworth Estate and therefore rather an unnatural sort of place with a somewhat oppressive feel to it. One's memories of Petworth usually consist of making painfully slow progress following a lorry through its streets. Neverless its attraction cannot be denied. William Cobbett wrote: "The park is very fine, and consists of a parcel of those hills and dells which nature formed here when she was in one of her most sportive moods. I have never seen the earth flung about in such a wild way as round about Hindhead and Blackdown, and this park forms a part of this ground. From an elevated part of it, you see all around the country to the distance of many miles. From the south-east to the north-west the hills are so lofty and so near that they cut the view rather short; but for the rest of the circle you can see to a very great distance".

The Walk

Distance: *Allow 3½ hours for this walk; the distance is 7 miles.*

Walk down the lane through the village and by the old red telephone box, take the footpath to the right which goes steeply down the hill. Pass through the five-bar gate, and past the old pub sign, over a stone footbridge and continue on in the same direction. You will come to a fingerpost sign where you are joined by a path from the right – at this point bear left, go down the concrete steps and over the small wooden footbridge. Here you will see another junction of footpaths where you should bear right. At the next footpath junction, bear left up the bracken-covered hillside toward the detached houses on the crest of the hill.

When at the top of the hill, you will cross another footpath – here proceed straight on using the stile to follow the path around a small estate of houses until you meet Grove Lane. We now need to find our way through Petworth town centre to the Midhurst Road on the west side of town. Probably the quickest way is to turn right on Grove Lane and then left into Rosemary Lane where you pass the court and police station. Towards the end of Rosemary Lane, take the path which runs parallel on the right hand side. At the car park, bear left and follow the pathway around until you arrive at the roundabout at the junction of the A272 and A285.

Take the A272 (Midhurst and Petersfield road). Very soon you will be offered the option of a public footpath on the left to take you away from the bustle of this road.

Take this path, passing through the swing gate. This public footpath has been properly left (at the time of walking) unploughed – perhaps the 1990 Rights of Way Act is beginning to have an impact! The path proceeds as straight as an arrow in the general (southerly) direction of the South Downs ahead of you and more specifically towards the small copse, where you turn right for 150 yards on a roughly surfaced road and then bear left, again heading in a generally southerly direction.

You will meet a bridleway (Rotherbridge Lane) where you should turn right. Eventually the lane swings to the left and descends to Rotherbridge Farm. Here you may meet two Labrador-type dogs who bark a lot, but seem to be friendly enough. Our route now turns right avoiding the crossing of the River Rother (although you may wish to stand on the bridge and enjoy the river). Pass through two gates in quick succession and then a further five-bar metal gate which takes you from an open field leading down to the banks of the Rother to a track with hedgerows.

At the disused farm buildings known as Perryfields, bear left and skirt around them and walk parallel with the Rother for a short distance. The river and path gradually diverge. Pass through disused gate posts at the end of the copse and

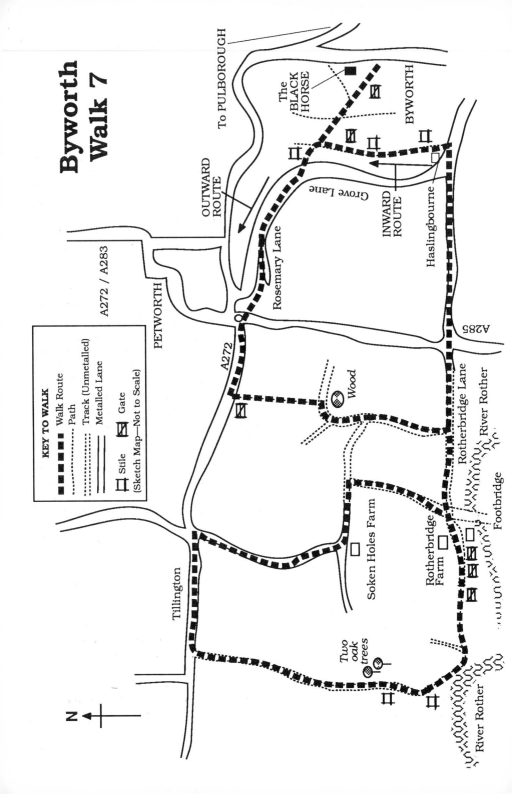

Byworth
Walk 7

N

To PULBOROUGH

The BLACK HORSE

BYWORTH

OUTWARD ROUTE

Grove Lane

INWARD ROUTE

Haslingbourne

A272 / A283

PETWORTH

Rosemary Lane

A272

A285

Wood

Rotherbridge Lane

River Rother

Soken Holes Farm

Rotherbridge Farm

Footbridge

Tillington

Two oak trees

River Rother

River Rother

KEY TO WALK

■ ■ ■ ■	Walk Route
. . . . .	Path
- - - - -	Track (Unmetalled)
———	Metalled Lane

Stile   Gate

(Sketch Map—Not to Scale)

bear right of the ditch before the open fields, climb a stile (which may be concealed) and head northwards on a wide, slightly sunken trackway with overhanging hazel trees. Climb a stile and then turn half left to walk under two oak trees that have seen better days. Continue on in the same direction until you reach the A272. Here, turn right and walk for about ½ mile into Tillington and then take the lane on the right (opposite the turning for Upperton).

Follow this lane as far as Sokenholes Farm where you bear left on a way that becomes sandy. After roughly 400 yards bear right to walk along a very sunken way to its end. At this point you will meet Rotherbridge Lane again and, for a short distance, re-trace your earlier steps. At the pair of cottages where we joined Rotherbridge Lane, continue straight on until the A285.

Cross this very busy road with great care and follow the quiet country road for about ¾ mile. Turn left and walk up the drive of Haslingbourne, climb the stile made from a five-bar wooden gate.

At this point I found the route initially difficult to follow due to some 'foul play'. For example this field was 'down' to cereal with the footpath illegally ploughed out. Difficulties were compounded by the lack of a fingerpost upon entry to this field and lack of a stile to take an exit from the field. My best advice is to walk in a direction parallel with the left-most power line – the step of the stile currently points in the direction that you should initially walk. At the other side of the field (alonside a power line pole) you should take your exit from this field. However no stile is provided and unless this situation has changed, you will have to climb through a loose barbed wire fence. These points have been reported to West Sussex County Council (together with the electric fence that follows). If action has been taken you may have an easier time than I did; if not let me know!

Walk along the edge of the field with the copse on the right – here I had to negotiate an electric fence – and you will come to a stile and fingerpost sign which enables you to cross into the field at your side. Walk (with the fence on your left side), climb the hill and walk toward the large five-bar gate with stile beside. You will soon find yourself back at your outgoing route, where you descend the hill through the bracken and re-trace your steps until you see the sign of *The Black Horse* alongside the footpath.

My thanks are due to Mr and Mrs D Chandler who kindly tested this walk for me.

Maps
*Landranger 1: 50 000
Sheet 185
Pathfinder 1: 25 000 Sheet
SU 42/52 & SU 62/72
Map Reference of
Start/Finish SU615278*

8 · A Downland Walk from *The Fox* at Bramdean

Background to the Walk

This walk takes us through a good mixture of arable land, open downland and parkland belonging to Hinton Ampner House. We pass the source of the River Itchen, and pass a battlefield where a great deal of blood was shed, but more of that later. Though one of the longer walks of the series, it is gentle with only one short, fairly steep path that climbs out of Cheriton up to the downs. It is a very open walk and strikes me as a good one for late spring. In a similar fashion to the Tichborne Walk (Ch. 11), you will find that the footpaths in the area on the north side of the A272 are badly marked.

Pub Facilities
Food is available at most times. Children are not allowed inside the pub but there is an outdoor garden where they may play. Dogs are not permitted inside the pub. Walkers are requested to avoid parking their cars in the pub car park. The pub has a payphone, serves real ale and has real fires in the winter.

Bramdean has some lovely old houses, and has given Winchester a pavement from a large Roman Villa found at Brookwood Park.

This walk takes place, close to the site of the Battle of Cheriton Down. The battlefield is now commemorated by a memorial stone erected 332 years after the battle took place. It was a battle that

How to get there
The Fox lies alongside the A272 (Petersfield to Winchester Road) at Bramdean. Travel by bus is possible – Hampshire Bus Service No. 67 will take you there from either Petersfield or Winchester.

The Fox at Bramdean.

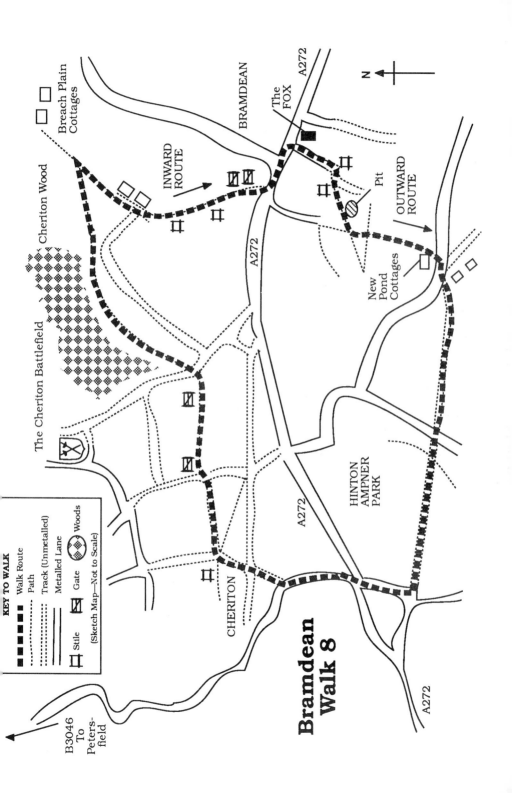

Bramdean
Walk 8

KEY TO WALK

- ▪▪▪ Walk Route
- ········ Path
- ········ Track (Unmetalled)
- ───── Metalled Lane
- ⊞ Stile ▩ Gate ✿ Woods

(Sketch Map—Not to Scale)

N

B3046
To
Peters-
field

The Cheriton Battlefield

Cheriton Wood

Breach Plain
Cottages

BRAMDEAN

The
FOX

A272

INWARD
ROUTE

OUTWARD
ROUTE

Pit

New
Pond
Cottages

A272

A272

A272

CHERITON

HINTON
AMPNER
PARK

Sunken Lane at Bramdean.

changed the course of the civil war and was a decisive defeat for the Royalists commanded by Lord Hopton, inflicted by the Parliamentarians under Sir William Waller. The latter was flushed with success from engagements at Alton and Chichester and morale was good. The roundheads occupied the high ground at Cheriton Wood and the cavaliers who were based in Cheriton, tried to dislodge them. There were about 10,000 men on each side and they fought for hours before a cavalier officer led his men along a sunken lane in an offensive charge. Waller's forces had expected this and raked the lane with artillery fire and used his own cavalry to attack the shattered horsemen. Hopton mounted a rescue operation to cover the retreat of his footmen and artillery.

Lamborough Lane was said to have run with blood and over 2000 soldiers lost their lives. The defeat for the Royalist armies was a significant turning point as it put an end to Royalist occupation of Kent and Sussex and also relieved the armies of the Earls of Essex and Manchester for future offensive operations.

The Walk

Distance: *Allow 3¼ hours for this walk; the distance is 6½ miles.*

There are two minor lanes running on both sides of *The Fox* – take the one on the right side (looking from the main road). You will pass a white, thatched house on your right as you start to climb the hill. At the end of the lane, on the right, climb the stile and after only 20 yards climb a further stile that takes you into the field.

Walk toward the right hand side of the small group of trees in the middle of the field (actually an old pit of some sort). Continue on in the same direction until you find the corner of the field that takes you into the next, arable field. Follow the footpath, as indicated by the yellow arrow on the stile, at the right hand edge of this field until the boundary drops back on the right – at this point take another path diagonally left. You will come to a junction of wide, open routes; proceed virtually straight on here (slightly left) heading south. You will soon see New Pond Cottages in the distance, which is your immediate destination.

Join the lane by turning right, passing the cottages and follow it for a few yards. Where the lane swings sharply right, leave it by continuing in the same direction with a forlorn house on the right and the farm buildings away to the left. You will now follow this track for ½ mile until you meet a road lined with magnificent beech trees. Cross this road and continue on for a further ½ mile ignoring footpaths on both sides and enjoying the views of Hinton Ampner House. You will eventually meet the Kilmeston Road on a sharp bend.

Turn right here and walk toward the A272. According to my O.S. Map, the area on the left should be the highest source of the River Itchen. Until recently it supplied several households with their own water supply. There was trouble though, back in 1954 when the water from one old cottage with a very deep well, that had always proved reliable and capable of keeping adjacent houses supplied, suddenly became tainted with a paraffin taste.

There are signs of past wetness here, with reeds and a watercourse but at the time of walking, in January, it was as dry as a bone and seems, rather like the River Meon's source at East Meon, to have dried up in recent years, possibly due to greater water extraction combined with drier weather. On the other hand that old county guide book *Arthur Mee's Hampshire* gives the source of the Itchen as Bramdean from whence we have just come. However, by the time you cross the A272 you will find water absolutely everywhere.

Cross the A272 and follow the B3046 towards Alresford for a mile or so. Where the road swings to the left, continue straight on up the drive marked 'no through road for vehicles'. The drive then becomes a sunken trackway as you ascend the downs again. Keep straight on at the first crossing of tracks continuing to climb until you reach the crest of the hill. Turn right here; not on the footpath into the field, but on the trackway between the fields (you touch the corner of a another walk in the series here – the one from *The Tichborne Arms*).

The views from this track have probably remained unchanged for the last fifty years. There is very little to offend the eye, just sheep and cattle grazing and the occasionally report of a shotgun in the distant woods. Cross the next track – you leave the Wayfarers Walk here – and walk through the next small five-bar wooden gate to join the path that runs along the right hand side of the field.

About ½ mile north of this point is where the Battle of Cheriton Down occurred. A small detour will take you there. It is difficult to imagine such a bloody battle in a peaceful scene such as this.

At the edge of Cheriton Wood you will come to a further small wooden gate; pass through this, cross a wide track, swing right and then immediately left to walk parallel with the wood about 30 yards away. Walk this route for about ¾ mile until you meet the point where the wood comes out to meet you.

Bear half right across the field, diverging from the wood by about 30 degrees or so. At the edge of this field, meet the boundary on its corner, touch a track also on its corner and then bear half left to follow the line of the hedgerow in front of you. This is an ill-defined path, unmarked and difficult to decide which side of the hedgerow it follows. You start off by following the right (south) side of the hedgerow until you cross a track where you switch to the left (north) side for the last few yards until you reach the junction of paths marked by the yellow arrows.

Turn right here, and walk on the right side of the hedgerow to pass Marriners Farm. Join a driveway at Marriners Farm for a very short distance and then leave it on its corner to head across a small field. The path brings you up to a hedgerow and then continues on the right side of the hedgerow. At the next boundary you will come across two bars that purport to be a stile. Bear slightly left and walk to the corner of the field that protrudes inward slightly. When you reach this, continue walking in a similar direction with the hedgerow on the left toward the clocktower ahead of you.

Climb the stile and walk past the tennis court on the left through the grounds of Bramdean House. I felt a little uneasy at this point as one does, when walking through a large private garden. I stopped to chat with the gardener who was mulching some small trees – a most professional man who obviously enjoyed his job and took a great pride in his work. He removed my doubts by confirming that the route was correct and then chatted about the many small trees in this part of the garden. He seems to know the age and variety of every one. He also volunteered that the house was built in the 1760's and extended, I think, in 1810 and 1910. The clocktower on the right, he went on to say, is intended to be a focal point of the gardens. With a feeling of guilt at not having done the things to my little garden that he was doing to his, I pressed on.

Turn half left after the court, toward the wooden-gate-with-stile that has a further tennis court beside it. Walk down to the A272 between two lowish flint walls, turn left and return to *The Fox* at Bramdean.

My thanks are due to Cliff Barlow who kindly tested this walk for me.

9 · A Walk on the Open Downs Above Owslebury

Maps
Landranger 1: 50 000
Sheet 185
Pathfinder 1: 25 000
Sheet SU 42/52
Map Reference of
Start/Finish SU512232

Background to the Walk

If you are a stranger to Owslebury, you will not know how to pronounce the name of this village. It is certainly not pronounced as it is written – 'Owslebury'. I have heard it said with the first two syllables rhyming with bustle, but most Hampshire folk that I have met, and who have an opinion on the subject, seem to prefer a rhyme with 'jostle'. So, if you say 'Ostlebury', you will not go far wrong.

Sticking to the subject of this name for the moment, it would appear to have a rather peculiar meaning. According to Richard Coates in his book *The Place-Names of Hampshire* it is an Old English (Anglo Saxon) word meaning 'blackbird fort'. Although it is a hilltop village and its physical situation may be responsible for the 'fort' part of the meaning, examination of local maps does not reveal any earthworks that could have given rise to the name.

The village itself sits comfortably on its hill, dominated by the church which stands high and

Pub Facilities
The Ship Inn
Food is available at most times, although currently on Sunday mornings only rolls are on sale. Children are welcome and there is an outdoor area where they may play in the summer months. Dogs are permitted in at least one area of the pub. Walkers are welcome to park their cars in the car park if they patronise the pub before or after their walk. The pub has a payphone available, it serves real ale and has a real fire.

How to get there
Owslebury lies about 8 miles south east of Winchester set back from the Corhampton/Winchester road. It is served by one bus service (from Winchester) – the Hampshire Bus Company Service No 33.

The Ship Inn, Owslebury.

57

Owslebury Church.

Alternative facilities
The Shearers is another inn on your route; a romantic and apt name for a downland pub. It looks humble, old and interesting, but unfortunately time has not allowed me to sample its qualities.

looks across to Southampton. It could not be described as a picturesque village, as it has houses of many styles – from terraced council-style houses to large old, timber-framed cottages. But this, and the football pitch you pass when entering the village, proves that the heart of Owslebury still beats and it is not (like so many Hampshire villages), a middle class, middle aged desert of neatly tended front gardens, devoid of rural Hampshire character.

The Ship Inn is a joy to enter. The current licensee always makes a stranger feel welcome. The pub is old with the main bar area heavily beamed (both the beams and their supports are timbers salvaged from a seventeenth century ship). The red-tiled floor that lies by the very large fireplace, forms the route from front door to bar and has been worn away with the passage of thirsty souls over the years. The main bar area is set back from the fireplace and is simple and homely with a relaxed feel. Shiny wooden tables, wheel back chairs and built-in cushioned wall seats add to the cosy snugness. There are many old photographs of the local worthies who have played for Owslebury Cricket Club and of Hampshire teams of times past.

The Walk

Distance: *Allow 4¼ hours for this walk; the distance is 8½ miles.*

From The Ship Inn car park, turn right and continue along the lane with the buttressed wall on the right and proceed down the steep hill. At the junction with Hensting Lane, turn right and after about 300 yards take the left fork to avoid the route back to Owslebury; continue following the lane as it climbs steeply after passing the farm on the right.

At the junction, marked by a brick and flint house that is a peculiar mixture of old and new, carry almost straight on up the gravelled bridleway. This bridleway suddenly changes into a very wide and pleasant green track. This effectively runs along

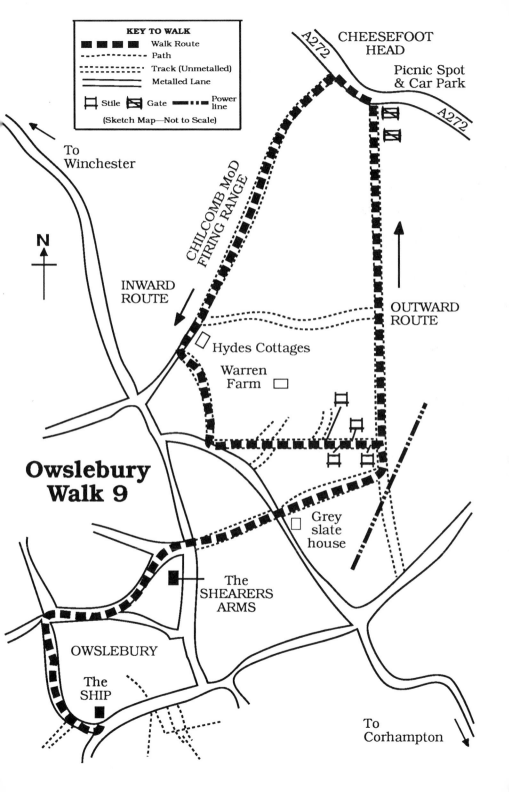

KEY TO WALK
- ▰ ▰ ▰ Walk Route
- -·-·-·- Path
- ⋯⋯⋯ Track (Unmetalled)
- ── Metalled Lane
- ⊟ Stile ⊠ Gate ▰·▰·▰ Power line

(Sketch Map—Not to Scale)

CHEESEFOOT HEAD

A272

Picnic Spot & Car Park

A272

To Winchester

N

CHILCOMB MoD FIRING RANGE

INWARD ROUTE

OUTWARD ROUTE

Hydes Cottages

Warren Farm

Owslebury Walk 9

Grey slate house

The SHEARERS ARMS

OWSLEBURY

The SHIP

To Corhampton

the bottom of a shallow valley; it crosses the busy Corhampton/Winchester road by a grey slate house and then continues onward in a very pleasant fashion, cooly shaded by a good selection of hazel, ash and crab apple trees many of which are covered in ivy.

This bridleway continues to follow the bottom of the shallow valley for a considerable distance. Turn left a little before you reach the power lines and follow the bridleway uphill. You eventually emerge into more open countryside in a new plantation, to follow a track made from broken rubble.

Pass the small white gate, alongside larger gates and carefully cross the very busy A272 to gain access to Cheesefoot Head – a convenient half-way place to picnic if you wish. Follow the A272 for a very short distance and take the first bridleway to the left that heads off in a south-westerly direction for the second half of the walk.

[If you wish to avoid crossing the main road to get to Cheesefoot Head the following alternative directions will suffice: Just before Cheesefoot Head turn left at the white gate keeping the fence and hedgerow trees on your right. Follow the path to the corner and turn right. At the white post fork right leaving the post on your left. Carry on to a fingerpost marking cross paths where you turn left to head in a south-westerly direction].

You now walk for a mile on very open downland and then join a gravelly track with a small wooded area on the right. This area to the right of your route is part of Chilcomb MOD range, and this land is out of bounds when the red flag is flying. However, the route that you are actually walking on is a right of way at all times, although on some firing days you may be held by a sentry until he has radioed through to ensure safe passage. The track becomes a surfaced lane by Hydes Cottages and you must follow this for 150 yards – at this point take the bridleway off to the left. This can be slightly overgrown, but remains reasonably walkable throughout most of the year.

You emerge briefly again at the busy Corhampton/ Winchester road before immediately turning away from it along the track as indicated by the footpath fingerpost sign, gradually diverging from the road. After just under half a mile, you will cross the track to Warren Farm – continue onward in approximately the same direction and you will come to a point where the track swings sharply to the left. Here, leave the track by taking the stile into the field on the right. Walk in the direction of the yellow arrow on the stile post toward the far side of the field. As you cross the field you will become aware of a small rectangular enclosure effectively forming an annex to the main field. At the far right corner of this you will find the stile.

You will discover that in fact there are two stiles which you should climb in succession and then bear half right toward the left-most (there are two) white pipe line marker on the opposite boundary. The stile that we need is about 20 yards to the right of this. Climb the stile, turn right and you will find yourself back on your original outward route where you should re-trace your steps back to *The Ship Inn*.

Thanks are due to Cliff Barlow who kindly tested this walk for me.

10 · Downland, River and Railway from *The White Lion* at Soberton

Background to the Walk

Maps
Landranger 1: 50 000
Sheet 185
Pathfinder 1: 25 000
Sheet SU 61/71
Map Reference of
Start/Finish SU610168

Like so many of the villages that we visit in this series, Soberton is notable for its homely pub and splendid church.

The White Lion is two pubs in one, with a local pub for the drinkers on the left and a townies pub for the eaters on the right; which is perhaps as it should be. The local pub (the public bar) is a cosy sort of place; made so by the fireplace that dominates the room by being angled towards its guests and lighting up the faces of those that are there in the winter. Bare floor-boards, yellowing walls, wooden pews, large wooden beams and bulging ceilings; these are the bones of the pub. A landlord of cheerful countenance with a sharp wit, with an artist in the kitchen; these are the flesh. There are other adornments of lesser importance; an old pew, a large scale Ordnance Survey map (which all walkers like to see) and several indentures in old-fashioned handwriting that I can never be bothered to read.

Pub Facilities
Food is available at all times. Children are welcome and are allowed in the lower end of the lounge bar. There is an outdoor area where children may play. Dogs are permitted if the pub is not too busy. The pub does not have a car park – patrons tend to use the lane but this is narrow. There is a payphone opposite. The pub serves real ale and has real fires in the winter months.

The White Lion, Soberton.

How to get there
Soberton lies in the Meon Valley on the other side of the river from Droxford and the A32. The area is served by the Portsmouth-Wickham-Droxford Bus Service (Southdown Portsmouth No. 38).

One thing that I did spend some time reading was the take-away menu (not that there is any take-away food, it is the menu that you take away). Somewhat unusually, it lists up and coming events over a three month period and makes significant claims about the merits of *The White Lion*. It describes the difficulties of Hampshire folk in finding a good pub in the county (something I have not personally experienced) and of their continuing disappointments. "All they wanted was a characterful and traditional country tavern, with a good beer and wine list, a menu that wasn't predictable or pricey, and the sort of friendly service and atmosphere that is often promised...but rarely delivered.....Now there's a fairly perfect pub in Hampshire. And that's no fairy tale..."

Soberton Church.

And now to more serious matters – the church. A fine, imposing building, situated perfectly with downland pasture sloping away from the south side. It has one of those attractive alternating stone and flint chequerboard towers that are more usually found in the villages surrounding Salisbury Plain. In the various Hampshire travelogues that I have consulted about Soberton, they all talk about the carving of the key and bucket on the tower. These, they say, are there because the butlers and other local house-servants contributed £70 to the restoration work in 1880. I expected these to be placed prominently at eye level, but they are so high up as to be hardly visible – and the bucket looks more like a purse. However, at the base of the tower, on the same face, is a plaque that reads :"This tower originally built by servants, restored by servants 1881". There is an old Roman coffin on the south side of the church that was dug up at Manor Farm in 1880 and in the churchyard there is a 1783 gravestone that asks passers-by to "shed a bitter tear" for a sailor, sadly murdered on the Hambledon road.

Inside there are too many treasures to list; old wall paintings, beautiful stained-glass windows, many brass memorials recording the sad losses of local people; there is one that tragically records four lost sons and a son-in-law in the Great War.

This is an extremely varied walk, full of interest. You will walk the course of the old Meon Valley line – a branch line of the London and South Western Railway, follow the course of the River Meon, encounter pleasing downland turf and experience some of the most aggressive and offensive "trespass" signs in the county. No doubt, due to the number of folk that use the nearby Wayfarers Walk, the occasional rambler unavoidably loses his way, but that is no excuse for these signs. Why not a "please" here or a "thankyou" there? The only comforting thought is that, in the course and fullness of time these signs have the tendency to fall off and disappear! But more of this matter later.

The Walk

Distance: Allow 2½ hours for
this walk; the distance
is 5¼ miles.

From *The White Lion* head down the hill with the red telephone box on your left. A few yards beyond the telephone box, take the footpath, also on the left. At the time of walking, this path was overgrown and was hard going – in fact, a rather poor start to a walk. However, the path, which runs along the edge of a farmyard, is only about a mile long and you soon join a much better gravelled path, by climbing the stile. (If the route is too overgrown take the road shown on the sketch map as an alternative).

Continue along this path until you meet a metalled lane. Do not join the lane but take the footpath on your left by climbing the stile or using the gate. This field path heads almost due north, following the left edge of the field. Pass into a second field by climbing the stile, continuing in a similar direction. The fence that was accompanying you on your left now falls back; continue in the same direction towards the metal bar gate and stile that marks the point where we leave the field.

Join a grassy track (on its corner), by climbing the stile and effectively proceeding straight on. This joins a pleasant wide green track, known as The Driftway, which I believe is a name meaning that it was an old track used for driving cattle. Unfortunately you will have to leave this track sooner than expected using the footpath to the left. (My Ordnance Survey Pathfinder Map shows the path much further on, so there appears to have been a recent diversion).

Having taken this footpath, it eventually takes you to the corner of a paddock that juts into the larger field. Turn sharp left and follow the outer edge of this paddock toward the houses and gap in the hedge that marks your entrance to the road. Here, join the road by turning left and then after 20 or so yards take the bridleway to the right. This route takes you down into the base of the Meon Valley.

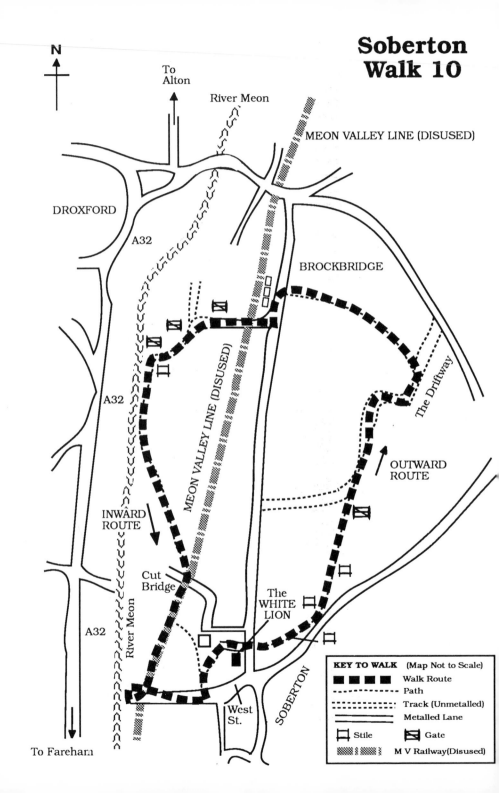

Soberton
Walk 10

N

To Alton

River Meon

MEON VALLEY LINE (DISUSED)

DROXFORD

A32

BROCKBRIDGE

MEON VALLEY LINE (DISUSED)

The Driftway

A32

OUTWARD ROUTE

INWARD ROUTE

Cut Bridge

River Meon

A32

The WHITE LION

SOBERTON

West St.

To Fareham

KEY TO WALK   (Map Not to Scale)

Walk Route

Path

Track (Unmetalled)

Metalled Lane

Stile   Gate

M V Railway (Disused)

At this point we need to turn south and are faced with a choice of routes: the old Meon Valley Railway Line or alternatively the Wayfarers Walk following the path that meanders alongside the river. This walk, makes the latter choice but does join the disused line a little later on, thereby achieving the best of both worlds.

Therefore cross the railway bridge, pass through the little gate and after about 50 yards pass through a similar gate quickly followed by a further one to head downhill to the River Meon. Immediately before the white footbridge, turn left by a large horse chestnut tree and climb the stile to follow the course of the Wayfarers Walk that takes you in a southerly direction, generally following the course of the River Meon.

Continue following the Wayfarers Walk – it gradually diverges from the river toward the beech and horse chestnut trees and approaches the old railway line by Cut Bridge. At this point you will see the aggressive and offensive signs that I mentioned in the introduction. Hopefully it will not be long before a further attempt is made to make these threatening signs illegal, as they tend to spoil the enjoyment of so many people.

The Meon Valley Railway.

By way of a short diversionary note, it is worth noting here that the warning 'trespassers will be prosecuted' is completely invalid. Trespass is a civil matter, not a criminal offence and the object of any proceedings is to compensate the landowner for any (unlikely) damages that may have occurred. This is why these signs are known among ramblers as 'wooden liars'. The late Tom Stephenson, the campaigner for greater access to the countryside, always quoted the following in response to a charge of trespass: 'We hereby give you notice that we do not, nor doth any of us, claim any right of way or other easement into or over these lands, and we tender you this shilling by way of amends'.

The irony of these signs is that they seem to suggest that the trespass must have some attraction and they therefore must be, to a certain extent self defeating. What delights might we find behind that sign? What are they trying to hide?

Climb the small rise to attain road height and then turn left to cross the bridge and take the steps on the far side to descend and join the route of the old railway. At the next bridge descend from the line using the path on the right, climb the stile and turn right under the arch into a narrow lane running alongside some picturesque cottages. Follow this lane until it brings you to a road junction. Here, take the footpath to the left across the pasture toward the church. You eventually leave this field by the narrow wooden five-bar gate to the right of the church, to return to *The White Lion*.

My thanks are due to Roger and Gillian Riley who kindly tested this walk for me.

11 · A Six Mile Walk from *The Tichborne Arms* at Tichborne

Maps
*Landranger 1: 50 000
Sheet 185
Pathfinder 1: 25 000 Sheet
SU 42/52 & SU 43/53
Map Reference of
Start/Finish SU572304*

Background to the Walk

Cheriton and Tichborne are dominated by the River Itchen as it rises and heads northward before it swings to the west to Winchester. I set off very early one January morning on this walk, and found that early winter mornings in the valley of the Itchen tends to bring layers of mist suspended in the air a few feet above the water. The villages themselves contain some lovely old houses; some thatched, some timber-framed, some built of a lovely warm, red brick.

The Tichborne Arms, our starting point, fits well into this peaceful background. Set slightly higher than the River Itchen that runs nearby, its gardens face southward making the thought of a warm summer lunchtime drink after the walk a delightful proposition. Its thatch hangs low on the road side of the building giving it a sleepy relaxed look.

For many hundreds of years, Tichborne has been, and perhaps always will be, dominated by the

Pub Facilities
Food is available at most times. Children are not permitted inside the pub, but there is an outdoor garden where they may play. Dogs are allowed inside. Walkers are welcome to park their cars in the pub car park providing they patronise the pub before or after their walk. There is a public telephone immediately outside the pub. The pub serves real ale and has real fires in the winter.

The Tichborne Arms.

How to get there
Turn off the A272 at New Cheriton on to the B3046 and head north and follow the signs to Tichborne. Travel to nearby Cheriton is possible by Hampshire Bus Service 67 from Petersfield and Winchester.

Tichborne family. There can hardly be a family with a more colourful and at times, tragic history in the whole of England.

The legend of the Tichborne Dole is well known and the charity still, I believe, carries on to this day. In the reign of Henry I, Sir Roger Tichborne's wife – a lady of wealth and great charity, begged her husband to set aside a some of money to create a dole for all who asked for it each year on Lady Day. She was nearing the end of her life and was bedridden. Sir Roger was clearly not a charitable person and promised her as much land as she could crawl around, while a firebrand stayed alight. She managed to encompass twenty acres and the field in the village is still known as The Crawls. After such an achievement, she ensured the continuity of the dole by placing a curse on the family if ever it was not distributed annually. Until 1894, 2000 loaves were distributed annually, but because of chaotic and unseemly scenes, money was handed out instead. In the last world war, Sir Anthony Doughty-Tichborne requested extra ration coupons to keep the the dole going. The Ministry of Food were initially receptive but changed their view when news leaked out of the proposal. Sir Anthony wrote to *The Times* and many bread coupons were generously sent from all parts of the country.

An even more prominent story of the Tichbornes was a claim to the title made by a Wapping butcher. Another Sir Roger Tichborne, went to South America in 1852. He embarked on a ship in 1854 to return to England but the ship went down with all on board. After a considerable time, and with leave to presume death granted, a new heir succeeded. Lady Tichborne, Sir Roger's mother, would not let the matter drop and continually advertised for him in both English and Colonial papers, also keeping a candle burning for him in his old room.

She eventually heard from a man trading as a butcher in New South Wales, who purported to be Sir Roger. The man was really Arthur Orton, a man of great daring and resourcefulness, who had contacted friends and servants to learn as much as possible of Sir Roger. The whole idea was really quite improbable as Sir Roger was small with sloping shoulders a narrow head and beaked nose, who had miraculously changed into a 24 stone giant of a man. She met him in Paris, swore affidavits that he was her son and promptly died.

The case ran for 102 days until a verdict was given against the claimant. He was then tried for perjury and after a further 188 day trial he was sentenced to prison for 14 years, but not before the action had cost the family £80,000.

It almost seems, perhaps not surprisingly, that the inhabitants of the beautiful villages of this part of Hampshire want to keep their countryside to themselves! This observation is brought about by the slothful way in which rights of way are marked in this locality. The minimum standards (fingerposting at intersections with highways), is just achieved, but very little else. This is a great pity as the area abounds with footpaths and bridleways open for enjoyment. From time to time therefore, you will have to be "on your metal" and follow these directions carefully.

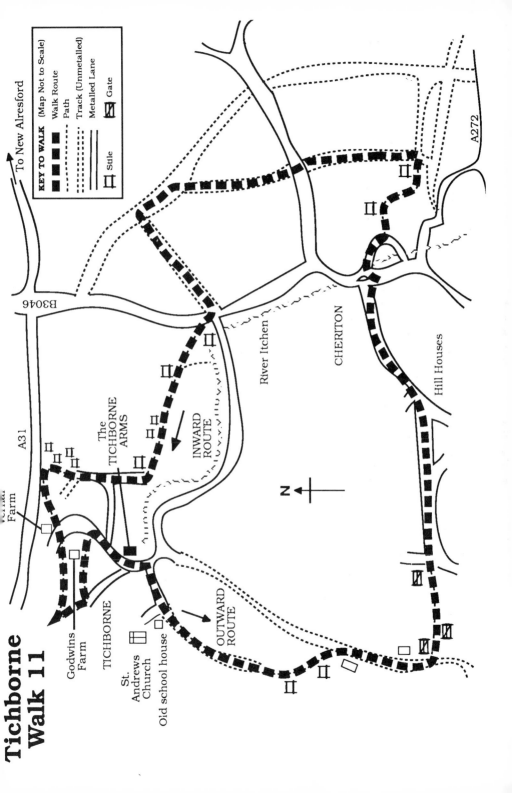

Tichborne
Walk 11

KEY TO WALK (Map Not to Scale)

▪▪▪ Walk Route
- - - Path
∙∙∙∙∙ Track (Unmetalled)
——— Metalled Lane
⌗ Stile   ▨ Gate

To New Alresford

B3046

A31

A272

River Itchen

CHERITON

Hill Houses

The
TICHBORNE
ARMS

INWARD
ROUTE

OUTWARD
ROUTE

Godwins
Farm

...Farm

TICHBORNE

St.
Andrews
Church

Old school house

N

Frost turns to vapour as the sun rises.

The Walk

Distance: Allow 3 hours for this walk; the distance is 6 miles.

From *The Tichborne Arms* turn left and walk up the narrow road (which soon takes a right-angle turn to the left), and then turn right, by the white timber-framed thatched cottage, up the lane to St. Andrews Church. The lane soon turns right, by the Old School House – bear left at this point and take the track between high hedgerows. The track then runs along the left hand side of the next field, initially in a gulley below the level of the field. Ignore the first (redundant) stile on the left and take the next one, turning half left and crossing the field diagonally toward the stile by the black farm buildings opposite.

Turn right here on a flinty trackway, effectively carrying on the south-westerly direction taken so far. Continue past the copse (on your right) and a small black barn on the left. Roughly 200 yards past the barn you will see a large pair of gates alongside a smaller gate for horseriders – pass through here. (The path here follows a different course from the current issue Ordnance Survey Map, but has been checked with Hampshire County Council). The route is ill-defined on the ground and the best instructions that I can give is to follow the line of the fence around to the left. This line will take you uphill towards the trees lining the top of the hill. You will spot a small wooden gate in the corner of the field that takes you into a copse.

Your route meanders approximately along the centre line of this copse avoiding trees that have fallen in the storms of past years. Take your leave of this copse by a gate that leads you to the corner of a narrow surfaced lane, beneath power lines where you should turn left. You will come to a junction (there is an isolated tennis court behind the trees here) where you should take the left route which is virtually straight on.

You will come across the pretty hamlet of Hill Houses; continue following the narrow lane until you come to Cheriton, where you should cross over the main road and follow the road opposite. Here, there are a few shops, a pleasant village green with perhaps more ducks than people. If you are in no great hurry, I am sure that you will enjoy a quiet stroll around the village but beware of the bridges. Each one, and there are many over the various branches of the infant Itchen, is labelled: "Take notice this bridge is insufficient to carry weights beyond ordinary traffic by order District Surveyor James Symes". Mr Symes has obviously not been in his post for many years and his name has now been painted over. It seems odd that he had his name displayed so permanently. Perhaps he thought that the bridges would have collapsed by now!

Turn left taking the small bridge towards the very attractive village school. Turn right, walking with the school on your left and take the narrow footpath (part of the Wayfarers Walk) just past Martyrwell. This takes you uphill between low wooden fences until you find yourself on high open downland.

Climb the stile and bear right, to follow the right hand boundary of this field through a ninety degree turn to the left until you come to a further stile. After climbing this, turn left onto a pleasant bridleway and after about ½ mile cross the Cheriton to Bishops Sutton byway. Continue onward – you will be joined by a further bridleway on your right. Your way broadens greatly at this point. Look for a Wayfarers Walk post on the right that indicates where you should turn sharp left and head down towards the B3046 and Cheriton Mill.

Turn right on the road for a few yards and take the footpath off to the left leaving the road by about 45 degrees and heading in the general direction of Tichborne Church on the horizon. There may be little trace of this path on the ground but when you reach the highest point of the field you will see the stile in the fence which is your target. After climbing this, bear half right and aim for the stile and gate marking your exit against the background of a strip of woodland.

There are in fact two stiles that you have to climb on each side of the woodland strip. Walk through the area of parkland with the cricket ground on the right toward the stile by the large iron gates. Climb the stile and take the drive away from the gates. After about 100 yards the drive turns sharp left to the Tichborne Road. We are now only a tantalising mile from *The Tichborne Arms* and this route over the stream was to be my route home. Many walkers seem to use it and were in fact using it on the day, but on subsequent checking I was disappointed to find that it is not a public right of way – so near and yet so far!

Therefore, instead of taking this sharp left, continue on for about 400 yards where you take a right hand fork. Go through some trees and follow the path with a fence on your left in open arable downland. A further 500 yards on are two stiles with a mini-conservation area on your right after which the fence continues on your right. Go over two more stiles, turn left and walk parallel with the A31 for a short distance; the path bears away from the road. This is a well-defined path with a fence on the left and a hedge on the right. After a small outcrop of fir trees pass Vernal Farm, cross the Tichborne road and follow the footpath up the hill with a hedge on the left.

A shepherd's hut on the downs above Tichborne.

At the intersection of footpaths and hedges, take the path that goes off to the left, keeping a hedge on your left. Go down the hill with Tichborne Church in view and in 300 yards or so take the path off to the left which goes through Godwins Farm. Turn right at the road and after a short distance you will be back at *The Tichborne Arms.*

My thanks are due to Cliff Barlow who not only kindly tested this walk for me, but also re-vamped the final part of the walk, when the route that I used to return home turned out not to be a public right of way.

12 · A Downland Ramble from *The Fox Goes Free* at Charlton

Maps
Landranger 1: 50 000
Sheet 197
Pathfinder 1: 25 000
Sheet SU 81/91
Map Reference of
Start/Finish SU889130

Background to the Walk

There are two possible explanations of the unusual name of this pub. It has been known as *The Fox* since at least 1750, but seems to have become *The Fox Goes Free* in fairly recent years. The simple version is that the name marks the reversion of *The Fox* to free house status. A more rustic and romantic view says that the name comes from the legend that the crafty Sussex foxes, by working in packs, completely bewilder the local Charlton Hunt.

Between 1670 and 1750 the Charlton Hunt was one of the foremost in England. It included among its members and visitors King William III, the Grand Duke of Tuscany and many dukes, barons and earls. The members of the hunt stayed at a small 'hunting box' know as Foxhall and no doubt, drank at the pub which was then known as *The Pig and Whistle*.

The hunt had two grand periods; before the Duke of Monmouth's rebellion and after the accession of William III. The master of the pack was Squire Roper, but he fled to France when Monmouth fell.

Pub Facilities
Food is available at most times. Children are welcome and are allowed inside – there is also an outdoor garden where children may play. Dogs are permitted in the pub. Walkers are welcome to park their cars in the car park, providing they patronise the pub before or after their walk. Their is a payphone available for customers use. The pub serves real ale and has real fires in winter. Overnight accomodation is available.

Alternative Facilities
On this walk you will pass by two other pubs, both in Singleton. These are The Fox and Hounds and The Horse and Groom.

How to get there
Charlton is signposted from Singleton on the main Chichester to Midhurst road.

The Fox Goes Free at Charlton.

73

On the accession of William III, Roper returned to Sussex and this led to a return of the hounds to their former glory and the hunt became supreme again.

Squire Roper died in 1715 at the age of 84 (in the field of course). The Duke of Bolton then became master until he became diverted by the charms of Miss Fenton, the actress. Finally there came the glorious reign of the second Duke of Richmond. The Charlton Hunt thereafter declined upon the death of the duke and in 1750 moved to Goodwood, changed its name to the Goodwood Hunt and died out at the beginning of the last century.

The most famous day of the Charlton Hunt was the epic chase of Friday January 26th 1738. E.V.Lucas in his *Highways and Byways in Sussex* gives an account taken fron an old manuscript, which begins thus:

"A FULL AND IMPARTIAL ACCOUNT OF THE REMARKABLE CHASE AT CHARLTON, ON FRIDAY 26TH JANUARY, 1738

It has long been a matter of controversy in the hunting world to what particular country or set of men the superiority belonged. Prejudices and partiality have the greatest share in their disputes, and every society their proper champion to assert the pre-eminence and bring home the trophy to their own country. Even Richmond Park has the Dymoke. But on Friday, the 26th of January, 1738, there was a decisive engagement on the plains of Sussex, which, after ten hours' struggle, has settled all further debate and given the brush to the gentlemen of Charlton."

Then follows a detailed account that runs to two pages, giving the detailed route of this struggle that started at 7.45 am in Eastdean Woods and finally finished ten hours and ten miles away at South Stoke on the River Arun. Here the 23 hounds killed an old bitch fox at 5.50 pm, having chased back and forth between Cocking, Westdean Forest, Graffham, Cowdray Park, Goodwood, Halnaker Hill, Eartham Common, Slindon Down and Houghton.

There was a subsequent attempt to restore Charlton to the centre of things and bring back some of the aristocratic custom to *The Fox*. A landlord in the 1880's, a retired CSM in the Royal Engineers advertised *The Fox* as "in view of Goodwood Racecourse, about one mile from the grandstand and one and a half miles from Singleton Station. First class accomodation for visitors. Bean feasts and private parties catered for."

The Fox also has a further claim to fame, far removed from the masculine world of the Charlton Hunt. It was the meeting place of the first ever Women's Institute group in England. It first met on the 9th November 1915, under the encouragement of the licensee of that time – Mrs F Laishley. There is a plaque recording the meeting.

The pub has a relaxed air about it, that no doubt comes from its having been there for 300 years. Obviously extended, the whole fits together well. The main bar has brick flooring, wooden tables, elm benches and a large brick fireplace. There is also a snug bar with a big inglenook fireplace. It is a lovely old pub with plenty of history that will provide a fitting end to your walk.

The Walk

Distance: *Allow 2 ¾ hours for this walk; the distance is 5½ miles.*

West Dean and then the Channel beyond.

Assuming a start from the pub, walk east (in the Singleton direction) for a few yards to the crossroads. Here, turn right into North Lane which is signposted 'to downs and bridleway'. After about 100 yards the surface of this lane becomes a flinty track that gradually winds uphill with high hedgerows and downs on either side.

Ignore the footpath off to the right, but approximately 250 yards further on take the bridleway off to the left that quickly starts to climb fairly steeply up Levin Down. As you near the top you will be faced with three fingerposts. At the first carry straight on and then look for the 'king sized' fingerpost commemorating the Charlton Hunt. There are inscriptions on the four sides of the post. Due to the natural effects of ageing, it is becoming difficult to read. On the front it says, "OLD CHARLTON HUNT" and on the other three sides of the post: "GHR 1972" "26 1738" "1918 AHS"

I suspect that the "1738" inscription refers to the epic day of the hunt described above, but I do not know the meaning of the other two.

At this point you should take the gate across the field – signposted to Cocking. Descend the hill with Broadham House on your left, and climb the hill on the other side. After the wood has accompanied you on the right for 200 hundred or so yards, you must be very careful to avoid the open gate in front of you – this is not a right of way – instead fork right, effectively following the western edge of this woodland of mature beech and young sycamore.

For just under ½ mile our route follows the edge of the wood and then swings into the wood and downhill. At the bottom you should avoid the possible left turn and carry straight on in the direction indicated by the bridleway sign. You will eventually emerge at a roughly surfaced track; bear left here keeping to the track for 30 yards and then turn off to the right on the bridleway until you come to the A286 road.

Unfortunately we have to bear left here and follow the main road for about 600 yards until the opportunity arises to leave by the public footpath on the right

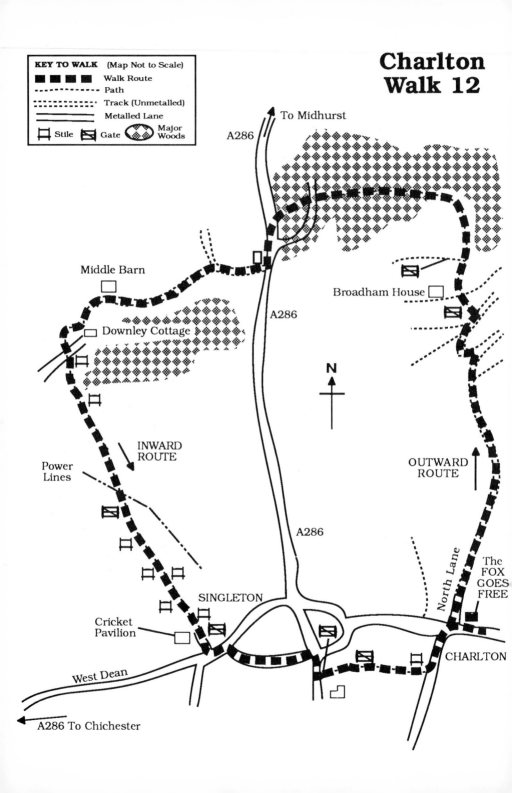

Charlton
Walk 12

KEY TO WALK (Map Not to Scale)
- ■ ■ ■ ■ Walk Route
- - - - - - - Path
- :::::::::::: Track (Unmetalled)
- ———— Metalled Lane
- 🔲 Stile   🔳 Gate   Major Woods

To Midhurst
A286

A286

Middle Barn

Broadham House

Downley Cottage

N

INWARD ROUTE

Power Lines

OUTWARD ROUTE

North Lane

The FOX GOES FREE

SINGLETON

Cricket Pavilion

West Dean

CHARLTON

A286 To Chichester

immediately after the flint house and barn. Pass through the sturdy brick pillars that were once part of an arch forming the small single line from Chichester to Midhurst that belonged to the London, Brighton and South Coast Railway. Avoid the right fork 200 yards or so after the demolished arch, continuing straight on, walking initially parallel with Wellhanger Copse on the left and then closing towards it.

As you pass Middle Barn do not turn off left into the woods but follow the outer edge of the wood with an open field on the right and head toward Downley Cottage in the distance. Zig-zag around the cottage and then join the track that climbs the hill through the young plantation. When almost at the top of the hill, bear half right and join a surfaced road for a few yards, before gaining access to the public footpath on the left by climbing the stile.

At the end of the first field, climb what remains of the stile and pass into a second field. Cross to the other side of the boundary fence by climbing the stile, but still continuing in the same direction. Pass under the power line, through a metal five-bar gate and climb the stile that marks a beautiful view of the valley below and Goodwood and The Trundle beyond.

Continue down the hill, walking slightly to the right of the pylon ahead of you, following the hedgerow on your right. Climb the stile in the bottom right hand corner of the field, carry on in the same direction to a further stile with some steps which again marks the site of the old railway line. Cross over the old trackbed to follow the elevated pathway, which could almost be described as a causeway. Follow this path which is beautifully lined with wild clematis until you reach the stile at the bottom of the hill (by a gate of peculiarly old fashioned 'shepherds crook' design). Climb a further stile that takes you behind the cricket pavilion, that marks Singleton Cricket Club's small ground. Leave the ground by the five-bar gate and cross the A286 at the post office by turning left – be very careful here as the visibility is not good and traffic is fast.

Bear right along the lane signposted to Charlton and turn right by *The Fox and Hounds* toward the church. Enter the churchyard via the gate and follow the path that runs along the north side of the church. Then leave the churchyard and pass under the covered walkway that belongs to No. 1 Church Way; continue on through a box-lined path and then through the swing gate into the field. Walk roughly parallel with the road away on your left – there may be markers in the field to guide you – until you emerge at the lane by climbing the stile and turning left to your starting point.

Thanks are due to Roger and Gillian Riley who kindly tested this walk for me.

Maps
Landranger 1: 50 000
Sheet 197
Pathfinder 1: 25 000 Sheet
SU 80/90 and SU 81/91
Map Reference of
Start/Finish SU938095

13 · Through Forest and Down from *The George* at Eartham

Background to the Walk

Eartham is a quiet, little-known hamlet that sprawls around the junction of two country lanes. It is dominated by beech trees that were at one time elegant, but now badly storm damaged and looking only a shadow of their former selves. Most of the buildings in the village are of flint and *The George* is no exception, sitting at this junction of ways alongside its colourfully painted sign showing St George's slaying of the dragon.

Pub Facilities

Food is available at most times (Lunch from 12.00 until 14.00 and Dinner from 19.00 until 21.30). Children are welcome both inside the pub and outside in the garden. Dogs are permitted and walkers may park their cars in the car park, providing they patronise the pub before or after their walk. The pub has a payphone available for customers use. Real ale is served and there are real fires in the winter.

It is a deceptively large pub, covered in creeper, that has clearly been extended from time to time over the years. Even today, on a bank holiday lunchtime, as I sit outside writing these lines, it seems to have a little room left inside in the bar. You enter a main lounge, where there is a restaurant at the back and a lounge on the right. The pub has its own beer – "Eartham Ale" on sale.

Eartham House (now Great Ballard School) was once the home of William Hayley, who succeeded his

The George at Eartham.

How to get there

From Chichester take the A285 to just beyond Halnaker. Turn off right where indicated to Eartham and keep following signs. Travel by bus is impractical as services from Chichester are very infrequent.

Eartham
Walk 13

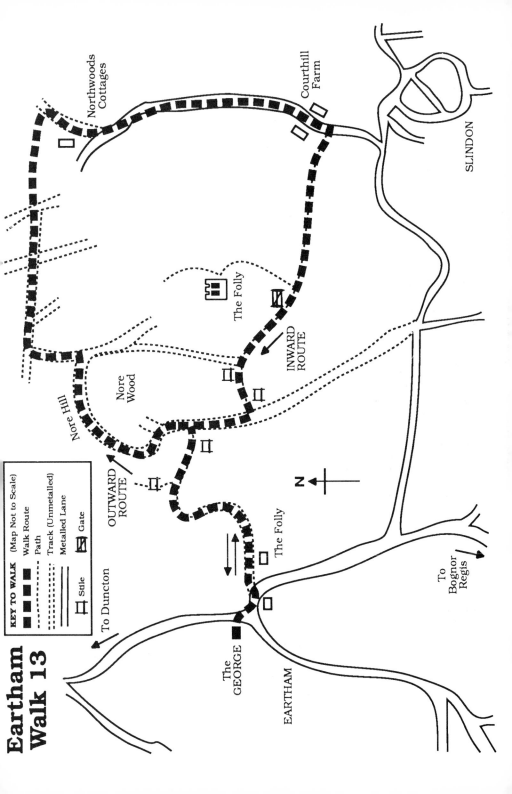

KEY TO WALK (Map Not to Scale)

■ ■ ■ Walk Route
▪ ▪ ▪ Path
⋯⋯ Track (Unmetalled)
—— Metalled Lane
🗖 Stile   🔃 Gate

To Duncton

Northwoods
Cottages

Courthill
Farm

SLINDON

The Folly

INWARD
ROUTE

Nore Hill

Nore
Wood

OUTWARD
ROUTE

N

The Folly

The
GEORGE

EARTHAM

To
Bognor
Regis

father as squire of Eartham and was the author of *The Triumphs of Temper*. He entertained many friends here, including Romney the painter and Cowper the religous poet, best known for his simplicity and tenderness. Cowper spent some time here looking after an invalid – Mrs Unwin, but the area was not completely agreeable to him as he wrote that "the melancholy wilderness of the scenes" were too much for him to bear. The countryside really belongs to that Sussex Man of Letters – Hilaire Belloc who has written so much in prose and rhyme about the area and who lived at nearby Slindon, as a child, and later at Courthill Farm.

The Walk

Distance: *Allow 2½ hours for this walk; the distance is 5 miles.*

From *The George* take the Bognor Regis road, passing Great Ballard Preparatory School. At the point where the road turns sharply to the right, turn off left – by some old farm buildings – along the track.

You will pass a small and well-built, old brick and flint Folly on the right. This track is flinty, firm, and even in wet weather has a firm base. Follow the path sharply to the left just after an old iron gate post.

If you look back here you should see on top of the hill behind Eartham, the impressive Halnaker Windmill; one of the oldest windmills in Sussex. It was built in 1750 for the Goodwood Estates and last worked in 1905. Hilaire Belloc who lived at nearby Courthill Farm, which we will pass later, wrote a song about the mill. It is rather sad and was written in 1914 just before the First World War and which was also the last year of his wife's life. He wrote it after driving past the mill and seeing it in ruins. It seems that the sight of the derict mill sent a shiver down his spine.....

....."H'anacker Hill is in Desolation:
Ruin a-top and a field unploughed.
And Spirits that call on a fallen nation
Spirits that loved her calling aloud:
Spirits abroad in a windy cloud.".......

The mill was restored in 1934 with a hand winder only, and is still in good condition.

After turning left, walk up the hill until you meet the gate and then turn right to walk along the left side of the field. Ignore the first stile in the fence on the left but use the stile in the corner of the field and immediately turn left on the bridleway. You will soon be faced with a fork; take the left route as indicated by the fingerpost. The route is now simple for just over half a mile – just keep following the obvious route – until you come to a public footpath.

Turn left here, heading north down the hill for about 300 yards or so. At the bottom of the hill you will be faced by a plantation known as The Plain. Turn right here on the bridleway. Look out for a fingerpost sign on the right; keep straight on here, ignoring the route that this fingerpost marks.

At the end of the plantation you will find yourself at a crossing of ways. Keep straight on to leave the wood and walk along the right hand edge of this field. As you leave this field, the route then becomes a fairly wide trackway between barbed-wire fences. After about 400 yards you will eventually come to a junction of paths – turn right here to walk along a wide trackway until Northwood Cottages. Here you join a metalled lane until you come to Courthill Farm. This is where the writer Hilaire Belloc lived for a short period in 1905 while he looked – together with his wife and five children – for his dream home which he eventually found at Shipley; there he bought a 14th Century house and a very large windmill.

The folly.

Just past the farm – where the road swings left to go up the hill to Slindon – turn off right onto the trackway. Follow this for about ¼ mile to an old farm building (you will see a folly over on your right). Continue straight on through the double gates and continue wending your way uphill on this pleasant track. The track swings sharply to the right and immediately afterwards turn left over the stile into the spacious field. Walk toward the far left corner of the field. Climb the stile to leave the field and turn right to join the bridleway. Take the first stile that arises on the left to enter a field and you will now be aware that you are on the original outward route. Return on this route to *The George Inn* at Eartham.

My thanks are due to Neil Pickett and Martin Furlonger who kindly tested this walk for me.

Maps
Landranger 1: 50 000
Sheet 197
Pathfinder 1: 25 000 Sheet
SU 81/91 and TQ 01/11
Map Reference of
Start/Finish TQ017115

14 · From *The George and Dragon* at Houghton

Background to the Walk

It seems almost mandatory that for an old pub to be worth its salt, it must have had a royal visitor. And so it is with the *The George and Dragon*; not only a royal visitor but Charles II no less, on his escape to France in 1651, after the Battle of Worcester. The best accounts say that he rested on the night of Monday, October 13, near Hambledon after meeting up with Colonel George Gunter of Racton, and at daybreak journeyed by way of Broad Halfpenny Down (the birthplace of cricket), and then via Catherington Down, Chalton Down and Idsworth Down to Compton Down. Continuing over the hills and descending at Duncton Beacon, the party had a narrow escape in Houghton Forest where they nearly met Captain Morley, the governor of Arundel Castle.

Their route then took them through Houghton and the King reputedly took ale at the inn and thus

Pub Facilities
Food is available at most times. Unfortunately, children are not allowed inside the pub but there is an outdoor garden where they may play. Dogs are permitted in the pub. Walkers may park their cars in the pub car park, providing they patronise the pub, but permission must be obtained first. The pub has a payphone available for customers use. Real ale is served and real fires burn in the winter months.

How to get there
Houghton is approached from the A29 Chichester to London Road and then the B2139 road to Storrington.

Other Facilities
The White Horse, advertised as the little pub with the big reputation, is on our route where we cross the A29.

The sun sets on The George and Dragon at Houghton.

fortified, he crossed the Arun to Amberley where he slept at the castle. On the South Downs at Amberley Mount, the King's horse threw a shoe and this was repaired at Lee Farm at Barpham from where he rode onward to Brighton to reach Fécamp on 16 October. That is the story as the Amberley folk will tell it.

According to Brigid Chapman in her book *West Sussex Inns*, (a goldmine of interesting tit-bits), around the turn of the century a circus stopped at the pub and the performers went in for a drink. The one exception was the elephant who, of course could not pass through the door. The landlord thoughtfully leaned out of an upper floor window and supplied the elephant with a bucket of water. There are, I believe, pictures of this happening still on display in the bar.

If you have time after your walk, Amberley is worth a visit. It has, of course, its Chalk Pits Museum next to the railway station. Here you will find (assuming it is unchanged from when I visited it) displays of local crafts and industries including quarrying, lime burning and a working printer, a potter and a black-smith. The bridge that you cross to get to Amberley is very old, like many on the Arun and West Rother and was restored by the bishops of Chichester in the fifteenth century. One of the great painters of Sussex scenes lived at Amberley in a beautiful thatched cottage in the village itself. Edward Stott showed, as so eloquently put by E.V. Lucas, "how the clear skin of a Sussex boy takes the light, and how the Southdown sheep drink at hill ponds beneath a violet sky, and that there is nothing more beautiful under the stars than a whitewashed cottage just when the lamp is lit". Close by is Amberley Wild Brooks; a wonderful name, conjuring up visions of winter-flooded fields, early morning mists and fowl everywhere. An often quoted story is that when an Amberley resident is asked where they live; in the summer they answer, "Amberley, where else would you live?"; and in the winter – "Amberley, God help us"; such is the wetness of the place.

The beautiful villages alongside the Arun also require a mention; Offham, South Stoke and Bury – a hamlet that once had the little boat ferry to Amberley, but which is now sadly defunct. On a fine summer day the "Arun valley" as I will call it, and the surrounding downland is one of the most beautiful places in England. I have no doubt that this walk will provide you with a most memorable day.

The Walk

Distance: *Allow 3½ hours for this walk; the distance is 6¾ miles.*

The South Downs Way, Westburton Hill.

Assuming a start at *The George and Dragon* car park, turn left onto the B2139 and walk down the road and turn right into South Lane. The lane is lined by beautiful thatched cottages – continue to the very end of this little lane and turn right onto the bridleway. Now you are about to have a frustrating experience! The route we need to follow travels slightly north of east, a few yards away along the river bank. The only way of gaining access to it without a minor trespass is to continue on this bridleway. Unfortunately this takes us in the opposite direction for 500 yards or so until we meet the junction of ways by an old gate post; here we turn back left and join the riverside path.

The Arun is tidal here and stays so until beyond Pulborough. Although this means a slightly less attractive river, it gives a pleasing extra dimension to our walk supplying the sight and calls of estuarine birds in addition to an already attractive habitat that provides the ghostly Grey Heron, Lapwing and normal lowland birds. This habitat coupled with the downs rising steeply away on two sides provides one of the most beautiful and varied habitats in the south country.

Initially this footpath is boggy and examining the winter undergrowth it looks as if it could provide a jolly good crop of stinging nettles in the summer months – my fingers are crossed for you! Continue to follow the river bank, crossing the odd small footbridge and stile, until you come to the stile at the immediate left of the old Amberley Bridge. Carefully cross the road here, climb the stile on the other side to rejoin the river bank to continue your progress along the Arun. Enjoyment of this peaceful pastoral environment is somewhat enhanced by the traffic that can be seen scurrying back and forth, on the roads high up in the hills around you.

Our route meanders, following the river towards the village ahead of us, which is Bury. As you near Bury you will cross four stiles and when almost alongside the church, bear half left leading to a lane that takes you past the church of St John the Evangelist and up through Bury. Continue on this lane over the cross

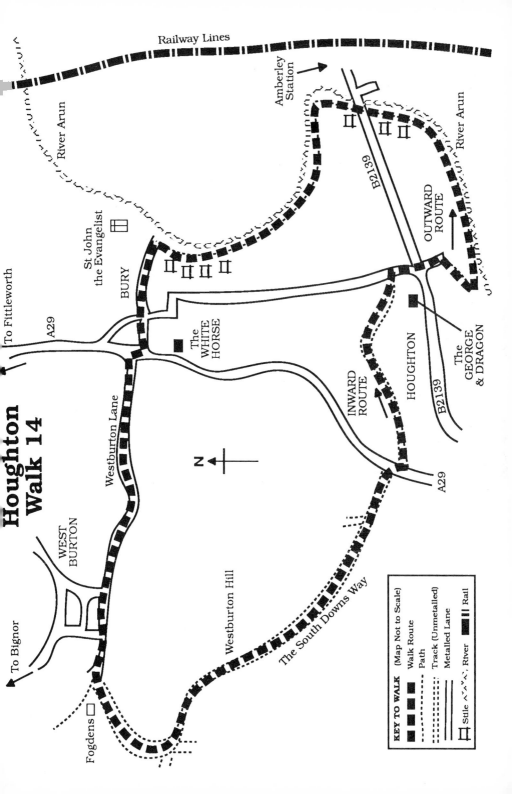

Houghton
Walk 14

Railway Lines

Amberley Station

River Arun

River Arun

OUTWARD ROUTE

B2139

St John the Evangelist

BURY

To Fittleworth

A29

The WHITE HORSE

HOUGHTON

INWARD ROUTE

The GEORGE & DRAGON

B2139

A29

Westburton Lane

N

WEST BURTON

To Bignor

Westburton Hill

The South Downs Way

Fogdens

KEY TO WALK (Map Not to Scale)

- Walk Route
- Path
- Track (Unmetalled)
- Metalled Lane
- Stile, River
- Rail

roads, passing the one-time house of novelist John Galsworthy (*Forsyte Saga*) (where he spent the last seven years of his life), and on until you meet the A29.

Cross the main road very carefully and proceed along Westburton Lane, a very quiet lane, in a straight direction for about a mile, ignoring all turnings until you reach the house called Fogdens, where you take the bridleway to the left.

This is a pleasant leafy way whose incline gradually increases. When at the top of the hill, by the three black barns, turn left and follow the South Downs Way. Little direction is required here, just follow the South Downs Way over Westburton Hill until you again reach the A29. Turn right and follow the A29 for a few yards until you have to cross (very carefully) and rejoin the South Downs Way.

If ever a view called for a wide-angle camera lens to capture the full magnitude of its beauty, this is one – the Arun lying as a sleepy snake below, the South Downs and the quarry at Amberley to the right, and further right the hills of Arundel Park.

Follow the chalky South Downs Way down toward the minor country road below, you will no doubt spot *The George and Dragon* at this point. At the road, turn right and climb the hill that takes you back to the village of Houghton. At the B2139 turn right for a few yards to return to *The George and Dragon*.

15 · A Short Crisp Walk from *The Richard Cobden Inn* at Cocking

Background to the Walk

There are, it seems, two ways of pronouncing the name of this village. Recently, I heard of an incident when a rather well-to-do resident of the area was asked for directions to the village centre. This dear old lady denied that the place existed until, when pressed, she eventually said "Oh you mean Kow-ing" (pronounced as if rhymed with towing).

Cocking, is on a very busy road but is surprisingly unspoilt. It is unfortunate that although you experience the best of the downs on this walk, you do not see the best of the village. As it is a short walk, you should have time to visit the church and stream, on the other side of the main road, so loved by W.H. Hudson the naturalist writer and praised in his *Nature in Downland*. This beautiful church is situated at the edge of the village, on high ground behind the stream. The church was originally built for the Benedictines and the tower and south aisle

Maps

Landranger 1: 50 000
Sheet 197
Pathfinder 1: 25 000 Sheet
SU 81/91
Map Reference of
Start/Finish SU878179

Pub Facilities

Food is available at most times and children are welcome both inside the pub and outside in the garden. Dogs are permitted in the pub. Walkers are welcome to park their cars in the pub car park, providing they patronise the pub before or after their walk. The pub has a payphone available for customers use. The pub serves real ale and has real fires.

Alternative Facilities

Cocking also has The Potter and Vine as a very suitable alternative.

How to get there

The richard Cobden lies on the main A286 Chichester to Midhurst Road. The area is served by Southdown Service No. 260 from Bognor Regis and Midhurst.

The Richard Cobden Inn.

were added to the Norman nave in the fourteenth century. The church has three medieval bells over 600 years old.

The name of this eighteenth century pub, our starting point, was changed to *The Richard Cobden* late in the last century. This was to commemorate the politician who was born in Heyshott nearby. There is also a memorial obelisk to him at Cocking Causeway, slightly north of this walk. His home was at Dunford House and he is buried in the churchyard of West Lavington church. In fact the area abounds with records of him.

If you, like me are guilty of mentally blurring together the names of William Cobbett and Richard Cobden, or not knowing too much of the latter then it might be worth a few moments to read a little of this great son of Sussex.

He is notable for his long campaign against the Corn Law and was founder of the Anti-Corn Law League. This action took 7 years to achieve success and led to a repeal of the laws which removed protection from domestic agricultural goods and brought the working man within reach of a decent standard of living. This had the effect of removing tariffs against foreign corn, so that free admission for manufactured goods from this country would be allowed into foreign countries. In retrospect, a sensible action for an industrial nation.

He was born in an old farmhouse at Heyshott not far away, in 1804. From Sussex yeoman farming stock, he was sent away to boarding school after his father had to sell the farm due to ill-fortune. The years at this Yorkshire school were miserable as it was a school similar in nature to Dotheboys Hall, that notorious creation of Dickens, based on schools of that period. He made up for the gaps in his education afterwards, by teaching himself French and other subjects.

He travelled the world in his early years and became a very successful businessman, but his career was never more to him than a means of independence. He basically stood for free trade and non-interventionist policies and firmly believed in a national education system. He worked almost wholly for free trade during the seven years, came close to bankruptcy and was only saved by public subscription.

Despite his strong views he overcame hostility with a quiet reasonableness with which he always spoke in the House of Commons. He was a realist in home policies and an idealist in overseas matters. His successful Corn Law campaign made him a national hero; his opposition to the Crimean War turned him temporarily into an outcast. Although always engaged in controversy, he never made an enemy and tragically during his life had less than his fair share of happy fortune.

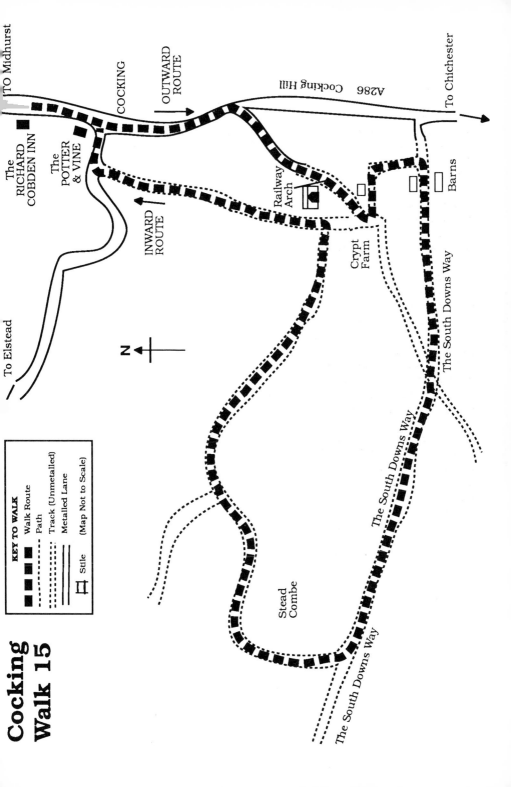

Cocking
Walk 15

KEY TO WALK

Walk Route
Path
Track (Unmetalled)
Metalled Lane
Stile   (Map Not to Scale)

N

To Elstead

To Midhurst

COCKING

OUTWARD ROUTE

The RICHARD COBDEN INN

The POTTER & VINE

INWARD ROUTE

Cocking Hill

A286

To Chichester

Railway Arch

Crypt Farm

Barns

The South Downs Way

The South Downs Way

The South Downs Way

The South Downs Way

Stead Combe

The Walk

Distance: *Allow 2 hours for this walk; the distance is 4½ miles.*

An old timber-framed cottage at Cocking.

I walked this route on New Years Day. It is very simple, short, easy and requires little instruction; and gets you up onto the downs very quickly. Just the type of walk to clear the head after a previous night's excesses.

From the pub, walk south along the A286 back into the village. You will pass *The Potter and Vine* at the cross roads. At the point where the main road swings to the left take the lane marked as a 'no through road' on the right and continue to follow this – you will be accompanied by a stream from a spring below you on the left. Pass under the railway arch and take the route off to the left at Crypt Farm.

This is a chalky track that winds uphill between high hedgerows. You will arrive at the South Downs Way (SDW) where you should turn right. Our route follows the SDW for some 1½ miles. A bridleway will cross the way in diagonal fashion – ignore this and turn right at the next right of way about ½ mile later.

Follow this byway gently downhill with the wooded slopes of Stead Combe on your right. Avoid the left turn that descends steeply down the chalky track, and continue straight on. You will find yourself at a junction of ways close to Crypt Farm. Turn left here, and walk between high hedgerows, joining a concrete track to meet the road.

Turn right and walk for a short distance to the main road where you should turn left and return to *The Richard Cobden.*

Winding downhill back into Cocking.

16 · A Short Easy Walk from *The Barley Mow* at Walderton

Background to the Walk

Maps
Landranger 1: 50 000
Sheet 197
Pathfinder 1: 25 000
Sheet SU 61/71
Map Reference of
Start/Finish SU788105

If I have the time and opportunity, I always enjoy a visit to *The Barley Mow*. It is a spacious pub with a pretty country garden, where it is most enjoyable to sit on a pleasant summer's evening with the downs not too far away. Inside, there are interesting collections of plates hanging on the walls and old bills of sale recording transactions between *The Barley Mow* and its brewery, dating back to the 1940's and 50's'. How did we cope with pounds, shillings and pence in those days?

For me, the most interesting feature of *The Barley Mow* is the skittle alley. Now, when I say skittles, I mean West Country Skittles – the best pub game of all, not any of the other inferior types. Where I come from, on the edge of Salisbury Plain, skittle alleys are ten a penny, leagues are active, and everyone is jolly because West Country Skittles is the jolliest of jolly pub games. Barracking, jeering and putting off the other team are all part of an evening's play. And it's a game where skill usually

Pub Facilities
Food is available at most times at The Barley Mow. One area of the pub is open to children and there is an outdoor area where they may play in the summer months. Dogs are permitted in at least one area of the pub. Walkers are welcome to use the pub car park providing they patronise the pub before or after their walk. The pub has a payphone available for customers use. Real ale is served and the pub has two real fires in the winter. There is a skittle alley available for hire throughout the year.

How to get there
This walk starts from the village of Walderton. From Emsworth take the B2148/2147, then B2146. Walderton is served from Chichester by Sussex Bus No. 54 on Mondays to Saturdays and No. 56 on Fridays.

Barley Mow, Walderton.

wins the day, but luck also has a definite influence, making it possible for all levels of player to make a contribution. The game is played with nine pins, with one (the king pin) being about an inch bigger than the rest. Three balls are used and they are usually made of lignum vitae or composition rubber weighing about 5lbs each, making it necessary for the fairer sex to sometimes throw with both hands.

Most of the skittle alleys in the south of England seemed to be viewed as a means of bringing in revenue, rather than for use by local villagers, with leagues few and far between. This is a great pity, but things will probably get worse, with the game disappearing altogether in response to the need for greater and greater financial return per square foot of floor space.

Anyone for skittles? (The Barley Mow, Walderton).

This is a short walk; ideal if you get off to a late start, say on a Sunday morning. It is over tracks and paths that are, on the whole, well drained, so it is suitable for summer or winter walks. As a lover of downland, I find that sometimes, for a change, I enjoy a walk at the foot of the downs, looking up and visually enjoying them in a way that is not possible from the ridge. In this fashion, there is a better perspective to be gained, and often, on a cold day when the wind is up, the relative shelter to be had is very welcome.

My original plan for the return leg was to descend the bridlepath through Watergate Hanger, and then take the bridlepath that runs roughly parallel with the B2146. This proved to be impossible as the route down through the hanger was blocked in many places, although I believe that this may have been cleared now. So instead of taking that route, a shorter alternative one was used along the south western edge of the hanger.

When I did this walk, it was one of those crisp winter mornings with some hazy sunshine, and mist laying in the valley. On this particular occasion, time did not allow one of those enjoyable visits to *The Barley Mow*, so I parked my car in the small patch between road and river immediately after turning off the B2146 – walkers often seem to leave their cars here, although it is not an official car park. I have noted its position with a 'P' on the sketch map. Wherever you park, please park tidily.

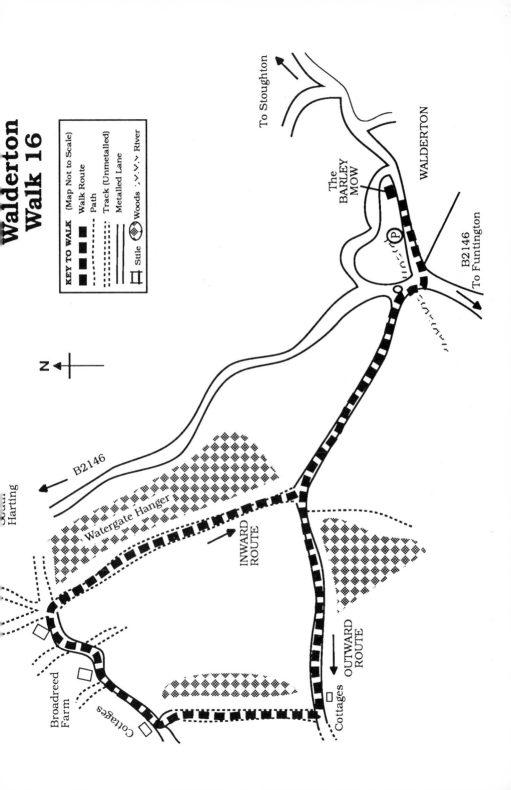

Walderton
Walk 16

KEY TO WALK (Map Not to Scale)

■■■	Walk Route
▪▪▪	Path
⋯⋯	Track (Unmetalled)
──	Metalled Lane
⊓ Stile	✿ Woods ∿∿ River

N

To Stoughton

WALDERTON

The BARLEY MOW

P

B2146
To Funtington

B2146

South Harting

Watergate Hanger

INWARD ROUTE

OUTWARD ROUTE

Broadreed Farm

Cottages

Cottages

Cottages

The Walk

Distance: *Allow 1¾ hours for this walk, the distance is 3¼ miles.*

Walderton – away in the valley below.

Cross the B2146 and walk northwards along the pavement. At the point where the B2146 swings to the right, bear left and follow the lane. This is an extremely pleasant metalled lane, that gradually climbs and winds uphill. Ignore the bridleway on the right and follow the metalled lane as it swings left.

You will probably see Racton Ruin in the distance at this point. Latterly notorious as a venue for 'house' parties, it seems to have had notoriety for almost all of its existence. It was built by Theodosius Keene for Lord Halifax in 1772 and was intended as a landscape feature and a gazebo. It was used as a summer pleasure house and gained a reputation as a resort of ladies and gentlemen of such ill fame that Lord Halifax is supposed to have ordered its destruction. It is also reported to have been used by smugglers for signalling to sea. As Lord Halifax occupied the post of President of the Board of Trade, and therefore not exactly a keen supporter of smugglers, this may have been another reason for its partial demolition.

Pass the pair of cottages (Woodlands Cottages) on the left and continue to the multi-fingered post where you turn immediately right and head north with an open field on your left and a thicket of mixed trees on your right. When you are faced with the next pair of brick and flint cottages, turn right onto the lane. Ignore the 'private no through road' sign, it does not apply to walkers. At the junction of routes by Broadreed Farm – bear right and walk with the low flint wall on your left. Having walked around the gardens of Broadreed Farm swing right, follow the lane – you will have a large beige coloured house on your left. The lane has hedges on either side. As you approach Watergate Hanger there is another pair of brick and flint cottages, turn right here and walk along the bridleway at the edge of the hanger. Continue following this track and it becomes chalkier and descends. Pause by the fingerpost sign and enjoy the views toward Walderton Down and Kingley Vale. A little further on and you will begin to re-trace your steps down Woodlands Lane back towards Walderton.

My thanks are due to Alan Hewlett and Sylvia Ricketts who kindly tested this walk for me.

17 · A Hike Around Hawkley Hanger

Background to the Walk

Some of this walk follows the old sunken lanes that abound in these parts. Although surfaced, these routes are only infrequently used by the motor car and provide easy relaxed walking.

This is without doubt, one of the best walks in this series and takes place in the very heart of The Hanger Country. The hangers are beechwoods that cling to the side of the chalk escarpment that stretches in a curve from Selborne via Hawkley to Steep. According to the academics, hanger is derived from the old Anglo Saxon "hangra" meaning "sloping wood". It would be more interesting to think that these woods gained their name because they literally appear to be hanging on to the hillside instead of merely growing out of it.

This stimulating countryside is made even more intriguing by the delightful and charming names that our ancestors have given to these slopes. We have Reston Hanger, Roundhills Hanger, Shoulder of Mutton Hill, Strawberry Hanger and my particular favourite Happersnapper Hanger. It is very distinctive countryside this; mostly chalk it is true, but an

Maps
Landranger 1: 50 000
Sheet 186
Pathfinder 1: 25 000 Sheets
SU 62/72 and SU 63/73
Map Reference of
Start/Finish SU748292

Pub Facilities
The Hawkley Inn.
Food is available at most times. Children are welcome in the pub and there is also an outdoor area where they may play. Dogs are also permitted in at least one area of the pub. Walkers are welcome to park their car in the car park providing they patronise the pub before or after their walk. The pub serves real ale and has a real fire in the winter months.

How to get there
Hawkley lies about 4 miles west of West Liss. Turn off the A325 at The Spread Eagle public house in West Liss in the direction signposted to Hawkley. At the time of walking, the Petersfield by-pass is having a great impact on the countryside around here and could mean a change in these travel directions. You will need to turn off left for The Hawkley Inn about mile after negotiating a hairpin bend.

The Hawkley Inn.

95

older darker chalk than that of the more typical downland areas of Hampshire, only a few miles to the south. This variance leads to hills with a steeper, more robust, almost muscular look, quite unlike the seductive feminine curves of normal chalk downland. In fact, when among the steepest slopes above aptly named Steep, the walker almost gains the impression of mountain foothills. A fact that has not gone unnoticed by tourists who have named the area Little Switzerland.

The countryside around Hawkley is prominently featured in local literature. William Cobbett passed through on his way from East Meon to Thursley in November 1822 and talks of the lanes with banks of white stone like Portland Stone. I hope that you will be as impressed with the countryside on your walk as he was on his rural ride of that day. He describes the hangers as "nearly perpendicular, and their tops so high in the air, that you cannot look at the village below without something like a feeling of apprehension. The leaves are all off, the hop-poles are in stack, the fields have little verdure; but, while the spot is beautiful beyond description even now, I must leave to imagination to suppose what it is, when the trees and hangers and hedges are in leaf, the corn waving, the meadows bright, and the hops upon the poles!"

"Till I came down to the Manor Farm".

Gilbert White was another local writer at nearby Selborne and a third local man of letters was Edward Thomas, who lived in Steep from 1906 to 1916. If a country area could ever be said to 'belong' to a writer, then the hangers belong to Edward Thomas. Almost wherever you wish to walk, you will come across a place, a hill, or a pub that he has written about either in prose or poetry. This walk is no exception. If you happen to walk along the lane at Priors Dean between church and manor house on a cold winter's day, then have these words from *The Manor Farm* written in the late winter of 1914, on your lips:

The rock-like mud unfroze a little and rills
Ran and sparkled down each side of the road
Under the catkins wagging in the hedge.

But earth would have her sleep out, spite of the sun;
Nor did I value that this gilding beam
More than a pretty February thing
Till I came down to the old Manor Farm,
And church and yew-tree opposite, in age
Its equals and in size. Small church, great yew.

Our base for the walk, *The Hawkley Inn*, is one of those pubs that gains in charm from a verandah giving it a vaguely colonial look. This feature is shared with another noteworthy pub; *The Harrow*, close by at Steep, now sadly debased by the Petersfield By-Pass. Always piled on the verandah at *The Hawkley* is a large stock of logs – a reassuring site on a cold winter's day, when returning from a misty walk around The Hangers.

Beyond these few words about the pub I have little to say about *The Hawkley Inn*; simply because, I am ashamed to say that I have not ventured inside. Time after time fate has conspired to prevent me from from passing the threshold. On two occasions in high summer I have returned from a walk around the hangers, with a gigantic thirst waiting to be quenched, only to find myself too early for opening time. Most recently, when writing this walk in fact, I was most careful to return in the evening, only to find it closed, this time for major refurbishment. It is now open again and spoken very highly of, but as Mr Murphy's Laws obviously operate very successfully in Hawkley, I have given up any hope of ever visiting the place and must leave this pleasure to you.

The Walk

Distance: *Allow just over 3 hours for this walk; the distance is 6¼ miles.*

From *The Hawkley Inn*, head downhill into the village, passing Hawkley's church, dedicated to St Peter and St Paul, set back on the right. This attractive old church is of Norman style, built in 1865 by Mr Maberley of Hawkley Hurst to a design of a Mr Teulon. An old map of the area interestingly states that the original bells were at one time stored in the village inn for safety from highwaymen.

At the green, bear left and after a few yards, turn right along the concrete drive (fingerposted Hangers Way). At the end of the concrete drive, follow the footpath that continues along the right hand side of the field following the line of a good-sized hedge all the way to the hanger, where at first you bear left and follow the perimeter of the hanger. At the fork, avoid the left lower route that takes you down towards the field and continue on the higher route, cutting into the hanger slightly.

Our route continues to gain in height, enabling the enjoyment of glorious views towards Oakshott Farm in the valley below; and beyond, Roundhills Hanger and Happersnapper Hanger. As we swing sharply away leaving the views, there is a fork in the route – avoid the left turn, continuing straight on. Eventually we leave the wood to cross a small section of field and after 200 yards or so you will

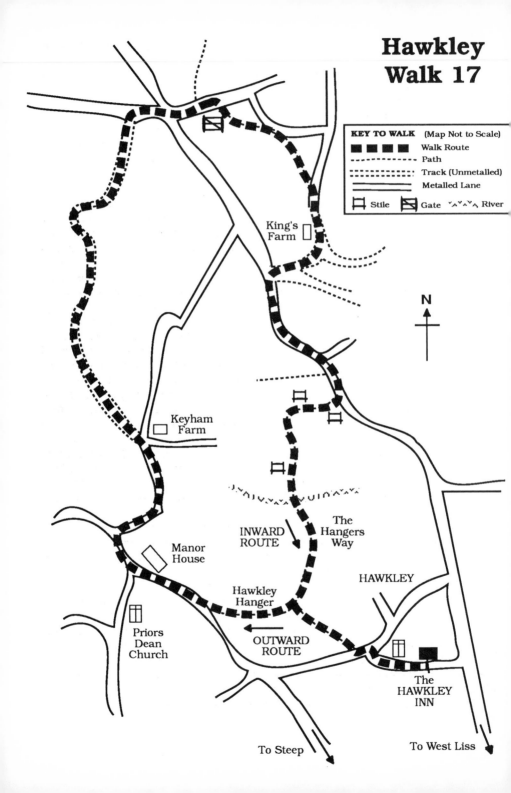

Hawkley
Walk 17

KEY TO WALK (Map Not to Scale)

■ ■ ■ ■ Walk Route
- - - - - - - Path
∷∷∷∷∷∷∷ Track (Unmetalled)
───────── Metalled Lane

🕳 Stile 🕳 Gate ᐯᐱᐯᐱᐯ River

King's
Farm

N

Keyham
Farm

The
Hangers
Way

INWARD
ROUTE

Manor
House

HAWKLEY

Hawkley
Hanger

Priors
Dean
Church

OUTWARD
ROUTE

The
HAWKLEY
INN

To Steep

To West Liss

enter the wood again. Follow the right hand edge of the wood until you arrive at the lane on the crest of the hill.

Turn right and walk between hedgerows of bracken to the (Elizabethan) Manor Farm and Priors Dean Church, which is, according to its plaque, of Saxon origin restored twice in recent times, once in 1857 and then 1982. It is, when viewed from the outside, a lovely old church, with an enormous old yew by the main entrance similar to the ones at nearby Farringdon and the rather more famous one that stood until recently at Selborne. The manor house is also of interest because of the covered way that runs for many yards from the house to the road, designed no doubt to keep visitors dry when alighting from their vehicle at the roadside. Unless you have deviated to visit the church, continue straight on by the manor house and after about 500 yards take the lane off to the right that leads you in a north-easterly direction. This lane winds its way uphill through overhanging trees.

When at the top of the hill, turn left on a trackway of generous dimensions that runs between hedgerows of bracken. This is the highest point of the walk, and there are good views to be had on a fine day. This track has a tendency to zig-zag a little, but stay with it until you descend to a lower level and bear right to join the East Tistead – Selborne road. Follow this over the crossroads and take the first footpath to the right (no fingerpost when I walked here) through a dilapidated gate – which at the time of walking had been taken off its hinges – to cross the field diagonally towards the left hand side of the small wood ahead of you.

Pass into the lane by turning right and walking for exactly 22 yards and then take the bridleway by the 'reserved game' sign. This way takes you through a narrow strip of woodland and you then emerge into open pasture to meet a very narrow lane where you turn right. Pass through King's Farm, ignoring the 'no through road' signs as they do not apply to walkers. Roughly a hundred yards beyond the farm, fork right and take the lower of the two possible routes (there was at the time of walking no fingerpost to guide you here). The route soon descends along a very narrow sunken track that eventually swings sharp right and joins the lane where you should turn left.

Descend the hill through the pleasant open woodland – ignore the little lane to Empshott – to continue straight on. Ignore the first right of way to your right, continue onwards for a further 200 yards or so and then take the footpath to the right over the stile to follow the Hangers Way again.

The footpath runs along the right hand side of this field, passing some old asbestos farm buildings on the right and through the stile or gate to pass into the next small field to take you to the foot of Hawkley Hanger. When at the right hand corner of this field you should turn left and continue following the perimeter of the field until you meet the stile. Descend the wooden steps, over the little footbridge and up the other side. You now follow the Hangers Way, along the foot of the hanger, needing no directions until you meet the point where you first joined the Hangers Way. Turn left here and re-trace your steps back to *The Hawkley Inn*.

My thanks are due to Peter and Robbie Moran who kindly tested this walk for me.

Maps
Landranger 1: 50 000
Sheet 197
Pathfinder 1: 25 000 Sheets
SU 81/91 and SU 82/92
Map Reference of
Start/Finish SU835207

Pub Facilities
Real home made food is
available at most times.
Children are welcome and
are allowed inside. There is
an outdoor garden where
children may play. Dogs are
permitted although the pub
has two dogs who often
wander in the pub. Walkers
who would like to park
their cars in the pub car
park while walking should
check at the pub before
doing so, due to possible
access difficulties. A good
number of people seem to
park on the road alongside
the pub.

Alternative Facilities
The Three Horseshoes at
Elsted is also on the route.

How to get there
Lower Elsted lies on a
country road due south of
Trotton which is on the
A272. The village is served
by Hants and Sussex Motor
Services No. 61 that
connects Petersfield, South
Harting, Stedham and
Midhurst.

18 · A Walk at the Foot of the South Downs from *The Elsted Inn*

Background to the Walk

Until recently, my walks in the downland area
around Elsted and Treyford cum Didling, always
started from Elsted vilage. If only I had ventured a
further mile or so along the road to Stedham, or if I
had not confused *The Elsted Inn* that people had
recommended with the 'inn in Elsted' I would have
spent the last few months as a happier man.

To come across this ordinary looking building
(more resembling a private house than an inn)
arouses interest but no more; unless that is, your
approach is down-wind of the kitchen. Then, you
will smell the soups bubbling, main courses being
cooked to perfection, and perhaps the whiff of syrup,
marking the preparation of some more of the best
treacle tart in the world. You will also realise that
you are approaching a rather special place, where
chips are unknown.

I am always reluctant to venture into print about
excellence or otherwise of a pub as it can create

Dusk falls at The Elsted Inn.

enemies. Also, a change of ownership can spell rapid doom, as there is no doubt that while structure and age provide the basis of a good pub, it cannot be a good pub without a good landlord. So, as of the 17th March 1991 let it be said this is a good pub, and hope that fate is not tempted by this statement to take a wicked twist.

You can't tell a book by its cover, so they say, and you certainly can't tell a pub from the outside. Enter this ordinary looking building and you will think that you are in a farmhouse parlour, with the old panelled walls and benches, large welsh dresser and blue gingham table-cloths. On the wall are sepia-colour photographs of old characters (I know not who they are), old racing cars and *The Elsted Inn*, back in the days when it was named *The Railway Inn*.

For a railway inn is what it was and that it is why it is here. Railway inns conjure up images of busy, impersonal, god-forsaken places with "saloon bar" engraved on the window. The fact that this particular railway inn of times past is nothing like this must tell us something about the sleepy, single-track country-fied nature of the Midhurst and Petersfield branch of the London and South Western Railway. It was constructed in 1864 and *The Railway Inn* was built almost next to Elsted station a little later. It must have had an interesting mix of custom in those days from its roadside and railside position. The railway was only a lightly used one and closed in February 1955.

The Elsted Inn has also had another, more recent name – *Ballards*. The Ballard family began brewing at their Sussex farm over thirty years ago. In the mid-1980's Carola Ballard and her husband Mike Brown opened *Ballards Pub* on *The Railway Inn* site and also started brewing in the stables. Due to its success, the brewery has now moved on again to Nyewood.

I am not sure who owns *The Elsted Inn* now; I have never asked. But it has an outstanding 'landlord' in Tweazle Jones who is the heart of the place and also has an outstanding chef. May it (and that treacle tart) long go on.

The Walk

Distance: *Allow 3½ hours for this walk; the distance is 7 miles.*

The Shepherd's Church, St. Andrews nr., Didling.

101

This walk takes place over land which in places is used for sheep farming. Please keep dogs on a lead when traversing these areas. From *The Elsted Inn*, turn back along the Elsted road, crossing the old railway bridge and turn left along the footpath opposite the cream-coloured Bridge Cottage. This is a tree-covered footpath that takes you to a gate marking the edge of an open field.

At certain times of the year it may be difficult to see which way to go, if illegal ploughing of the footpath has taken place. Initially take a line slightly to the left of the wooden pole supporting the power line. As you near the pole you will have to walk mid-way between the two poles and then aim for the gap in the fence on the opposite side of the field.

In this second field, have confidence and continue walking in the same direction. At the edge of this second field you will eventually see a rickety finger-post sign. Cross two large ditches at this point and take a well defined grassy route between two fields, that is lined by trees.

At the next junction of public ways, turn right – heading south in the general direction of the South Downs. You will walk through three fields passing through a five-bar metal gate at the end of the third field. When I walked this route, there were low electric fences across the route; easily crossed by an able-bodied adult, but none the less an obstruction and definitely illegal.

As you enter the field through the gate, walk toward the large oak tree. From this tree proceed half-left to the hedgerow and follow it to the stile, which takes you through the line of the boundary fence. Your footpath exit lies mid-way between the two houses at a small metal bar gate and track that takes you past The Old Cottage and down to the lane where you turn right. Our route now takes us along the footpath that leaves the lane to the right at Woolbeding Farm; but if you are fond of old interesting churches, then I strongly advise a visit to St Andrews, which lies a little further along this lane, (take the narrow lane that leads to the downs.

St Andrews is a most charming and small Early English church, where a pleasant experience is to sit on the churchyard seat early in the morning under the large old yew tree, and watch the sun rise from Linch Down, wondering, like I did, whether to scale the downs or continue at their foot towards Treyford. It was a most restful moment, warmed by the late autumn sun, listening to a laughing green woodpecker in nearby woods, a shrieking lapwing overhead and the background sounds of sheep.

Assuming that you are now back at the farm, take the path up the concrete drive into the farmyard, passing through the Hampshire Gate and past the rather isolated fingerpost toward the low corner of the field and through another Hampshire Gate. Walk along the right side of this field and negotiate a further two stiles, then continue to follow the right hand edge of this field that is lined by small oak trees. Cross a further stile to walk along the left hand edge of the next field, proceed down a steepish slope through a damp wooded area, cross the brook and climb the hill on the other side. You will join a grassy path between two banks that is part of the garden of nearby houses and join the lane by turning left into Treyford.

Elsted
Walk 18

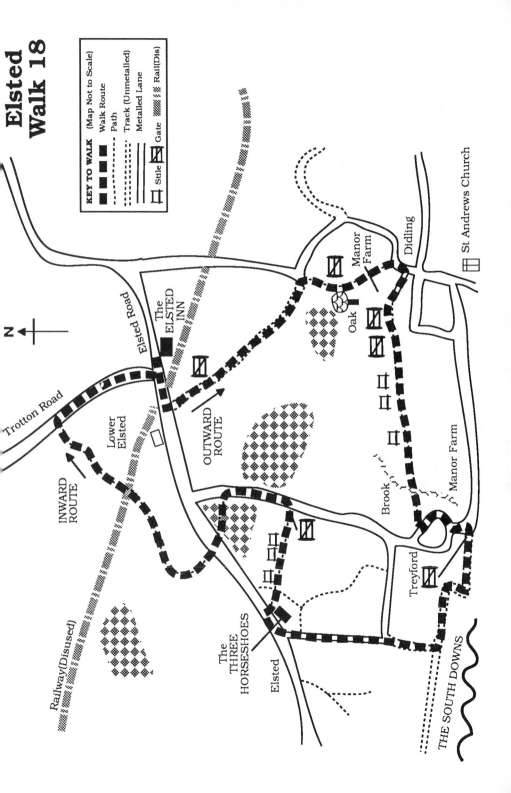

KEY TO WALK (Map Not to Scale)

- ▮▮▮ Walk Route
- ▪▪▪ Path
- ┈┈┈ Track (Unmetalled)
- ── Metalled Lane
- ⌸ Stile ⎍ Gate ▓▓ Rail(Dis)

N

Trotter Road

Elsted Road

The ELSTED INN

Lower Elsted

INWARD ROUTE

OUTWARD ROUTE

Railway(Disused)

The THREE HORSESHOES

Elsted

Manor Farm

Oak

Didling

St Andrews Church

Brook

Manor Farm

Treyford

THE SOUTH DOWNS

A charming signpost at Treyford.

You will meet a further road – bear left and pass Manor Farm House and join the bridleway off to the right by the bend in the road. There is a religous almost 'shrine-like' sign here, that makes a pleasant change, indicating the way to go, which is through the five-bar metal gate. This track runs along the rear of some very large properties and you should ignore all footpaths in either direction. You will soon enter more open land with the wooded slopes of Elsted Hanger to the left, walking between fences and then along the right side of the field.

Join a track which swings to the north and takes you back towards Elsted. Join the lane on its corner where you proceed straight on toward Elsted. At the village cross-roads turn right and at the sign of *The Three Horseshoes* take the steep drive through the area that is used as a car park by the local residents and wind your way down the concrete path resembling a private garden path that takes you between the bungalows and to the stile marking the field.

If you look carefully you should see a fingerpost in the opposite corner of the field. Here, you cross the narrow strip of land into the next field. Negotiate a stile and plank bridge, cross the corner of the next field and a further stile and bridge. Climb a further stile under the shade of an oak tree. Leave this large-ish field by a stile (next to a six-bar metal gate) that takes you into the road where you turn left.

Walk for about 700 yards and take the bridleway to the left through the copse. For some reason my companion, Sable, a rough collie, refused to walk through this wood and had to be carried the short distance to the Elsted/Lower Elsted road.

Cross the road and the narrow field and turn right, walking with the wood (Elsted Rough) on your left. This path initially follows the line of the road but eventually diverges away from this line – keep following it until you meet the Trotton road. Turn right here and return to the road junction marking the site of *The Elsted Inn.*

My thanks are due to Roger and Gillian Riley and Bert and Pat Morrisey who kindly tested this walk for me.

19 · A Short Ramble from *The Hampshire Bowman* at Dundridge

Background to the Walk

It was because I received so many warm reports of this simple isolated downland pub that I decided to set about finding it and to start a walk from there. It was a real discovery, and I was almost as enthralled as when I first found *The Royal Oak* at Hooksway, so long ago now that I do not care to remember.

If you approach Dundridge Lane from the fiveways by Corhampton Golf Club, your route will follow a winding single track road. The hamlet of Dundridge is a sleepy sort of place that you would have no reason to visit unless you were going to the pub. Very little traffic passes, as is made clear by the dog or two that may confront you on a hot summer's day, peacefully asleep in the road. *The Hampshire Bowman* rests by a simple T-junction and has a large gravelled car park and spacious lawn. The word that best describes it is 'unspoilt'. The impression gained when visiting for the first

Maps
Landranger 1: 50 000
Sheet 185
Pathfinder 1: 25 000
Sheet SU 41/51
Map Reference of
Start/Finish SU578184

Pub Facilities
At the time of writing, food is not available due to kitchen refurbishment, but catering will be resumed after Easter 1991. As the pub consists of a single room, licensing laws do not allow children inside the pub, but there is a large garden area where they may play in the summer months. Dogs are welcome in the pub. Walkers may park their cars in the pub car park providing they patronise the pub before or after their walk. The pub serves well kept real ales direct from a tapped barrel and a real fire is provided in the winter. There is no overnight accommodation available.

How to get there
Dundridge is situated about 3 miles west of the A32 at Droxford. The nearest bus services are at Droxford and are the Southdown (Portsmouth) Service No 38 Portsmouth – Droxford, and Southampton Citybus Service No 52 Southampton – Droxford.

Hampshire Bowman, Dundridge.

HEADQUARTERS OF THE PORTUGESE RACING SARDINE CLUB

So this is where all the decisions are made. Hampshire Bowman, Dundridge.

time, is of entering a room that has apparently not changed since the 1950's, or even earlier. It seems to have escaped the pressures to modernise and become just another mere 'outlet' for the fizzy products of a large brewery. There is no feeling of being processed or fleeced of your money, no taped music or noisy gambling machines. There is no one who is called 'my-name-is-Tracy-how-can-I-help-you', who although willing to help has no belief in the cause.

This is a place that might have been in William Hazlitt's mind when he penned those evocative words:

"How fine it is to enter some old town, walled and turreted, just at approach of nightfall, or to come to some straggling village, with the lights streaming through the surrounding gloom; and then, after inquiring for the best entertainment that the place affords, to take one's ease at one's inn".

On a hot summer's day time passes slowly here at *The Hampshire Bowman*. There is a quiet calm about the place and it provides cool shelter from the hot summer sun outside. The walls are yellowed, the furniture is rickety and the large wooden table is well-scrubbed. Interesting old documents line the wall; mostly indentures, but there is also a bill advising the hanging of several poor souls for murder, larceny and highway robbery.

The pub sells Gales Ales but in addition it usually has some Archers Bitter available. The name is very appropriate and you would be forgiven for thinking that it had been specially produced for the pub. This is not the case however, as Archers is a Wiltshire Brewery based in one of the old Swindon railway sheds and claims that the high vaulted ceilings and cool interiors are very conducive to quality ale production.

There is aways some mystery and intrigue about country pubs as isolated as this. For instance, in the early evening it is occasionally possible to spot an extra-marital assignation. The signs are usually self evident and the general course of events follow a similar pattern. A lady in her mid-twenties arrives, (in a shiny white 'soft top' car) at high speed and accompanied by a cloud of dust as she enters the car park. She is clearly not sure if she has found the right location and either sits in her car with fingers drumming impatiently or more probably enters the bar and orders a strongish drink. A period of extreme discomfort now takes place with watch-glancing, window-watching and frequent sipping. Relief will eventually occur when the second half of the newly formed partnership appears. The next stage is one of deep plotting in a hand-held huddle; plotting that is impossible to overhear. The whole scene is over soon with both players speeding off in opposite directions in one final cloud of dust. From the first dust cloud to the last hardly an hour has passed.

As a footnote to end these short notes, it is worth mentioning that the pub is not a complete backwater. Its importance must not be overlooked and a simple plaque reminds us that *The Hampshire Bowman* is the illustrious home of the Portugese Racing Sardine Club!

When I look back at this walk, I remember it as being mostly along unsurfaced lanes between high hedgerows; a walk that suddenly produces without warning, a most beautiful view of unspoilt downland, seen at its best with the setting sun behind. It was a hot late-summer day on my walk; yet another hot day in the long heat wave of the 1990 summer. There was a dry dusty smell in the nostrils that occurs after such periods from the cereal and hay in the fields.

Whatever the weather brings for you, I am sure that you will enjoy this excellent walk in this beautiful and quiet rural setting.

The Walk

Distance: *Allow 2¼ hours for this walk; the distance is 5½ miles.*

Dundridge. Down the steps into the valley.

From *The Hampshire Bowman* turn left and then immediately right along the country lane signposted to Bishops Waltham. After about half a mile you will see a footpath off to the right – ignore this and look for the footpath to the left 150 yards later.

Climb the stile to leave the road and take a route, that heads diagonally across the field toward the opposite corner where there is another stile. Turn left at this point where you climb the stile and then walk uphill, crossing the narrow field to the wood. You will now need to climb three flights of wooden steps after which you will soon meet the edge of this narrow strip of woodland. Take the footpath across the field and at the edge of the field you are faced with a small problem in judging the correct way! There are two possible routes here: one is a track continuing onward immediately in front of you, the other is a route winding around to the right between hedgerows. Take this latter route which eventually becomes a flinty track which serves as a drive to several houses.

You will soon meet a very narrow lane where you should turn left. After 200 hundred yards or so, by a house called High Bank your route degenerates again into a trackway with a very rough surface. At a T-Junction by a cattle shed keep straight on. Follow this track until you pass Jervis Court House and Farm and rejoin a slightly wider metalled lane. At the road junction marked by the fine old Scots pine trees in the middle of the island, carry straight on (signposted to Dundridge). At the next junction bear off to the right, by the post office letterbox and almost immediately turn left onto the flinty track to pass between Highfield Farm and Wyches Farm.

This track is of a pleasantly undulating nature and then narrows to become a route more resembling a footpath in nature. Swing sharply uphill by a timbered thatched cottage to come to the end of the track and turn left onto the lane.

Leave the metalled lane where it sharply turns right. This enables you to carry on in a similar direction on a lesser lane which is barely surfaced. Descend the hill and you will see a fingerpost sign among some yew trees pointing left. This is a particularly beautiful spot of downland and comes as a surprise after relatively flat country.

Take this path down the steep hill, using the wooden steps. At the bottom of the hill, at the point where you meet the open field, bear left and follow the fence that curves and separates the field from the steep downland. Follow the edge of the field until reaching the copse, where you pass across to the other side of the fence using the stile, and continuing on in the same direction, walking through the remains of the copse. This area seems to belong to that increasingly rare classification of unspoilt chalk downland. Follow the thick hedgerow on your right, to the stile some distance ahead.

Climb the stile and turn immediately right and walk for 50 yards toward the hedgerow where you turn left and walk with this hedgerow on your right leaving the field by the stile (by a green gate).

At this point we need to follow a footpath diversion recently agreed. Take this route to the left after the green gate, climbing with the hedgerow on the left through the copse towards the top of the hill. Turn right following the hedge on the left

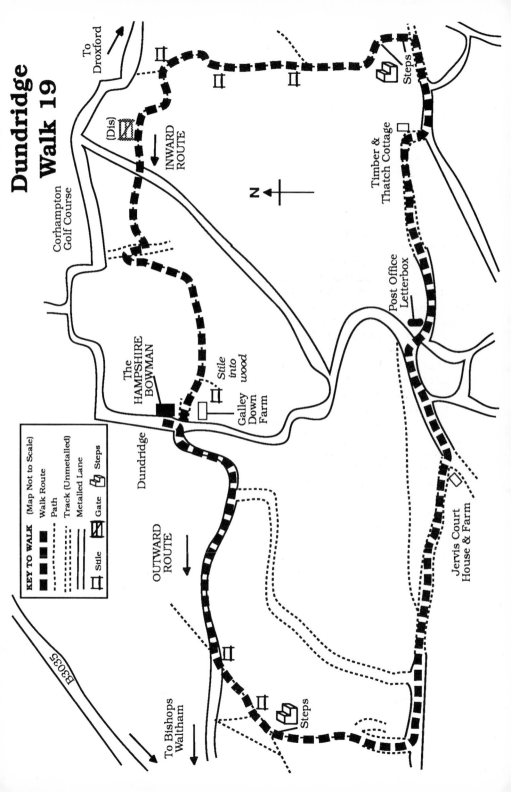

Dundridge
Walk 19

To Droxford

Corhampton Golf Course

INWARD ROUTE

(Dis)

Steps

Timber & Thatch Cottage

N

Post Office Letterbox

The HAMPSHIRE BOWMAN

Dundridge

Stile into wood

Galley Down Farm

OUTWARD ROUTE

Jervis Court House & Farm

B3035

Steps

To Bishops Waltham

KEY TO WALK (Map Not to Scale)

Walk Route
Path
Track (Unmetalled)
Metalled Lane
Stile Gate Steps

(There are fine panoramic views to the right). Follow fencing round to your left to the field gate and stile to the Corhampton Golf Course/Droxford road

Cross the road and continue on the bridleway almost immediately opposite. Follow this well-defined route swinging to the left through a strip of overgrown woodland. There is then a second section of path before you come to a spot where the way ahead is not immediately clear. Turn sharp right here – this path eventually descends quite steeply – until you almost meet the road where you bear left as indicated by the fingerpost.

Follow the left edge of this field having turned almost due south. Following the left edge of this field you will come across two stiles in quick succession. The next (third) stile would take you into the wood, should you climb it you will enter the wood. Avoid this stile, and instead turn right and walk down toward the left hand side of the barn. There is a very small stile here which takes you between the barn and a newish house (Galley Down Farm). Meet the narrow lane where you turn right to return to *The Hampshire Bowman*.

Thanks are due to Roger and Gillian Riley and Bert and Pat Morrisey who kindly tested this walk for me.

20 · Two Walks from The Red Lion Inn at Chalton

Maps
Landranger 1: 50 000
Sheet 197
Pathfinder 1: 25 000
Sheet SU 61/71
Map Reference of
Start/Finish SU732160

Background to the Walks

The downs in these parts have only a thin covering of topsoil and appear white when ploughed – hence the name Chalton with its Old English meaning of chalk farm. The spelling has taken several forms over the centuries, starting as Cealctun in the 11th Century, passing through intermediate Chaulton, Chalctone and Charlton to arrive at its present form.

One cannot pass through Chalton without being attracted by two features – pub and church. It is no accident that the two are so close together. In Chalton as in many other English villages, the pub was originally built as a workshop for the artisans employed on the rebuilding of the church. There are other examples of this in the south country, for example at Rudgwick near Horsham, where the pub is even closer to the church.

An excellent guide to St Michaels Church by the Reverent Ewen Pinsent is available from within; it is very readable and is much more than the normal dry, dusty old guide to ecclesiastical architecture. It

Pub Facilities
Food is available at most times. Children are welcome inside and there is also an outdoor garden. Dogs are permitted inside the pub. Walkers are welcome to park in the car park, providing they patronise the pub after their walk. The pub has a payphone, serves real ale and has a log fire in the winter.

Red Lion from Lychgate.

How to get there
Turn left off the A3M north of Horndean and follow signs to Chalton. There are no bus services to the village.

contains a lot of colourful information about the village as a whole, and I have taken the liberty of including one or two anecdotes from its pages in this chapter.

The Red Lion is supposedly the oldest pub in Hampshire, dating from 1147 and the site is also mentioned in Domesday. The pub's name comes from the crest of John of Gaunt who was once lord of the manor here. There are several stories associated with the pub that are worth telling. Many years ago it was the habit of a certain villager to hide up the chimney when a particular person approached. One day, to bring him down, someone had the idea of putting a bale of straw on the fire, to smoke him out! This was unsuccessful, and he was quite safe and well – he took advantage of an alcove inside the chimney where he was safe from the heat and smoke.

Another incident recounted in the church guidebook, took place after one of the village's "Club Days". Like neighbouring South Harting, the village had a benefit club which held an annual celebration; in Chalton's case this was always on the second Tuesday of July. On one particular occasion, some of the villagers refused to go back to work, and sat drinking ale in *The Red Lion*. To counter this, and to get the workers back to their haymaking, the farmer offered to pay for all the ale in the house, if the landlord would pour it all away. Fortunately the landlord would not do this and the men carried on with their drinking.

In more recent times, *The Red Lion* had a landlord who was one of the very best practitioners of the art of keeping good ale. Ron Stirzaker's bitter was renowned for miles around. It always had a superb nutty flavour not found elsewhere and was always so cool, clear and consistent. Perhaps it was his military background which provided the discipline that is, no doubt, required for good ale-keeping. Like all good landlords he placed great importance on the quality and cleanliness of the pipes between cask and pump. He made himself personally responsible for this, refusing to let even the brewery's technical department near his cellar.

Hilaire Belloc described Michell's Ale at *The Washington Inn* in Sussex as the most admirable and impossible-to-be-too-much-praised Cervisian nectar. He surely would have been equally enthusiastic about the ale at *The Red Lion*, and judging by the number of folk that still make the pilgrimage from miles around, I suspect that there is still something good on offer there.

These days, very few of the inhabitants of the villages of this part of Hampshire are natives of the area. One has to be comparatively wealthy to be able to afford a house in a village, and this means that townies come in and buy up the housing stock.

But there is still a certain commonality from village to village. Besides the farm workers that are still always to be found, there is of course the vicar, if not within the village, then certainly in an adjoining one that is part of the parish. Next comes the local publican, who in these days of increased disposable income, is usually more prosperous than hitherto. Then there is the village historian who is often a retired schoolmaster or officer of the armed forces. Of the creative arts, there is usually a potter to be found, or a writer or even a poet, inspired by the tranquility of the surroundings. I am reminded that this area is no exception as

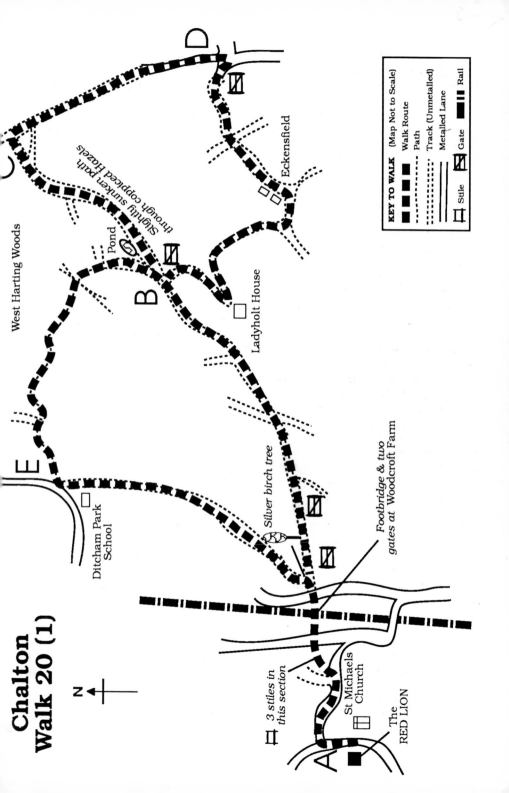

Chalton
Walk 20 (1)

N

West Harting Woods

Slightly sunken path through coppiced Hazels

Pond

B

Ladyholt House

Eckensfield

D

Ditcham Park School

E

Silver birch tree

Footbridge & two gates at Woodcroft Farm

3 stiles in this section

St Michaels Church

The RED LION

A

KEY TO WALK (Map Not to Scale)

■■■ Walk Route
• • • Path
••••• Track (Unmetalled)
──── Metalled Lane
■ ■ Rail
⊟ Stile
⌗ Gate

I have just re-discovered a charming book of poems entitled *Country Spread* by Mrs Lorena Trigg, a resident of neighbouring Finchdean (having returned from the Falkland Islands a few years ago). Half of the poems are of those windswept South Atlantic islands that were almost forgotten until a few years ago; the other poems are of the more gentle countryside of the south country that we are fortunate enough to enjoy. She has given her kind permission to reproduce some of her poem *Down a Country Lane* that so poignantly illustrates the beauty of these two walks:

"Down an old country lane let us amble,
(A lane carved by feet, hooves and wheels,)
Where hedges of dog-rose and bramble,
Stand guard around arable fields.

A tiny vole darts into hiding
Where leaves of wild scabious lie,
A bush cricket sits, softly chiding
At a large bumble-bee bumbling by.

We'll pass by an oak of fine stature,
Perhaps once a oakwood spread here,
A haven for many a small creature,
And home of red squirrel and deer........

So come, let us wander at leisure,
To listen and notice, with zeal,
Each season's collections of treasure
The country lane's proud to reveal."

Walk 1

Distance: *Using the 'figure of eight' design of this walk, three distances are possible. The long route (ABCDBEA) is 8 miles; the medium route (ABCDBA) is 6½ miles; the short route (ABEA) is 3 miles.*

Section AB

With *The Red Lion* on the left, take the small road toward the telephone box, and then join the lane by bearing right and climbing the hill. Follow this road and just before the crest of the hill, climb the stile and take the footpath off to the left, indicated by the fingerpost sign – the path takes a diagonal line across the field, diverging from the road at about 30 degrees.

Climb the tubular steel stile and walk down the hill diagonally across the downland turf to a further stile of the same pattern. Cross the road, and use the footbridge to cross the railway line, pass through the wooden pallet gate and then the six-bar metal gate. Cross the Ditcham Park road, and after a few more yards you will come to a junction of ways, by a silver birch tree. Take the route to the right of the tree, passing through a metal five-bar gate. Follow this pleasant grassy bridleway, until you come to a fork; here, take the left-most route enclosed by hazel and hawthorn trees.

At the end of this short enclosed section, you will pass through a small wooden five-bar gate, and then turn left onto the grassy way. You will shortly come to a rather open junction of ways – carry straight on here, keeping to the Sussex Border Path (SBP), and continue following the green grassy way.

Section BCDB

The SBP that we are following, then turns diagonally right away from the more obvious route (by a large 6-bar metal gate). You will pass a large man-made circular pond on your left, and then you will climb up through an old coppiced hazel wood, following a slightly sunken path. Continue following this path for just under half a mile until the last part of the climb, where you will walk parallel with the south east edge of the wood – about 100 yards away on the right.

You will emerge on to a green grassy way again – continue following this for roughly 500 yards. At this point, to be sure of staying on the SBP, you must take a left fork. This is very easy to miss as it is not fingerposted; the only way that I can describe it is to turn left by a silver birch tree. If you miss this point, it is of no real consequence as you will come to the 'CD' track anyway. Carry straight on for a further 200 yards or so and then turn right. (This point marks the end of our progress on the SBP).

Walk for about 250 yards and you will start descending a fairly steep hill on a gravelly track – you will probably glimpse Uppark House to your left. The last part of the descent is metalled. Bear right on to the bridleway, passing through the green metal six-bar gate. Continue on, walking along this gravelly track. At the next junction, continue following the indicated bridleway route by turning right. This track dips and climbs – you then have to bear left and then immediately fork right, following the left hand side of the wood. Pass through the tiny settlement of Eckensfield and then turn right along the gravelly track.

You will come to an open desolate spot – avoid the bridleway to the left and continue straight on towards Ladyholt, (you should see Ditcham Park School, on the horizon ahead of you), following the drive to Ladyholt House. Just before you get to the house, bear sharp right off the drive, almost reversing direction, and take the grassy track down through the woods back to the SBP.

Section BEA

Cross the SBP at Point B, bearing right following the open grassy track for 100 yards and then taking a fork to the left to stay on the bridleway. Your bridleway route then leaves the open grassy track and becomes more enclosed, accompanied on either side by silver birch trees. Cross a crossing track and after a 100 yards or so, you will find yourself in a green valley, and open downland for the first time on this walk. Climb the steep path at the edge of the wood, which zig-zags gradually up the hill toward Ditcham Park School.

At the point where you join the road, bear left and take the shingly route, past the school. The remaining route needs little description now as there are no turns to make until you arrive back at the point near Woodcroft Farm where you forked at the silver birch tree. From here onwards, merely retrace your steps back to the village of Chalton.

My thanks are due to Mr and Mrs D. Chandler who kindly tested these walks for me.

Walk 2

Distance: Allow 2 hours 15 minutes for this walk. The distance is 4½ miles.

From the Red Lion, turn left and walk up the short hill with the telephone box on your left. Turn right at the "Give Way" and walk up the hill passing the large farm buildings on your right. Just before you reach the crest of the hill turn left off the road, climb over the broken stile and follow the footpath across the field. At this point you will probably experience the driving gale that seems to blow permanently across the top of Chalton Down.

You will soon come to the next stile, after climbing this, walk diagonally left – in the direction shown by the plastic arrow on the stilepost – toward the railway footbridge and Woodcroft Farm below. Climb the stile at the bottom, walk toward the road and then turn left on to it for 30 yards and then right to the footbridge. Take care over the footbridge, the steps are mossy and are slippery when wet.

Walk through the "pallet gate", and then the six-bar metal gate, along the muddy track and around the right hand side of the red brick house, then take the bridleway on the right side of the silver birch tree, passing through a metal five-bar gate. This bridleway is identified on the map as Harris Lane indicating that it had greater importance at one time.

After roughly 400 yards the land on the right becomes wooded. Ignore the single bar gate and walk along the trackway that skirts the left hand side of the woods. This trackway is pleasantly wooded with the trees forming a natural archway for most of the way. At the small wooden bar gate carry on in the direction indicated by the bridleway and Sussex Border Path (SBP) fingerpost sign. The

Chalton
Walk 20 (2)

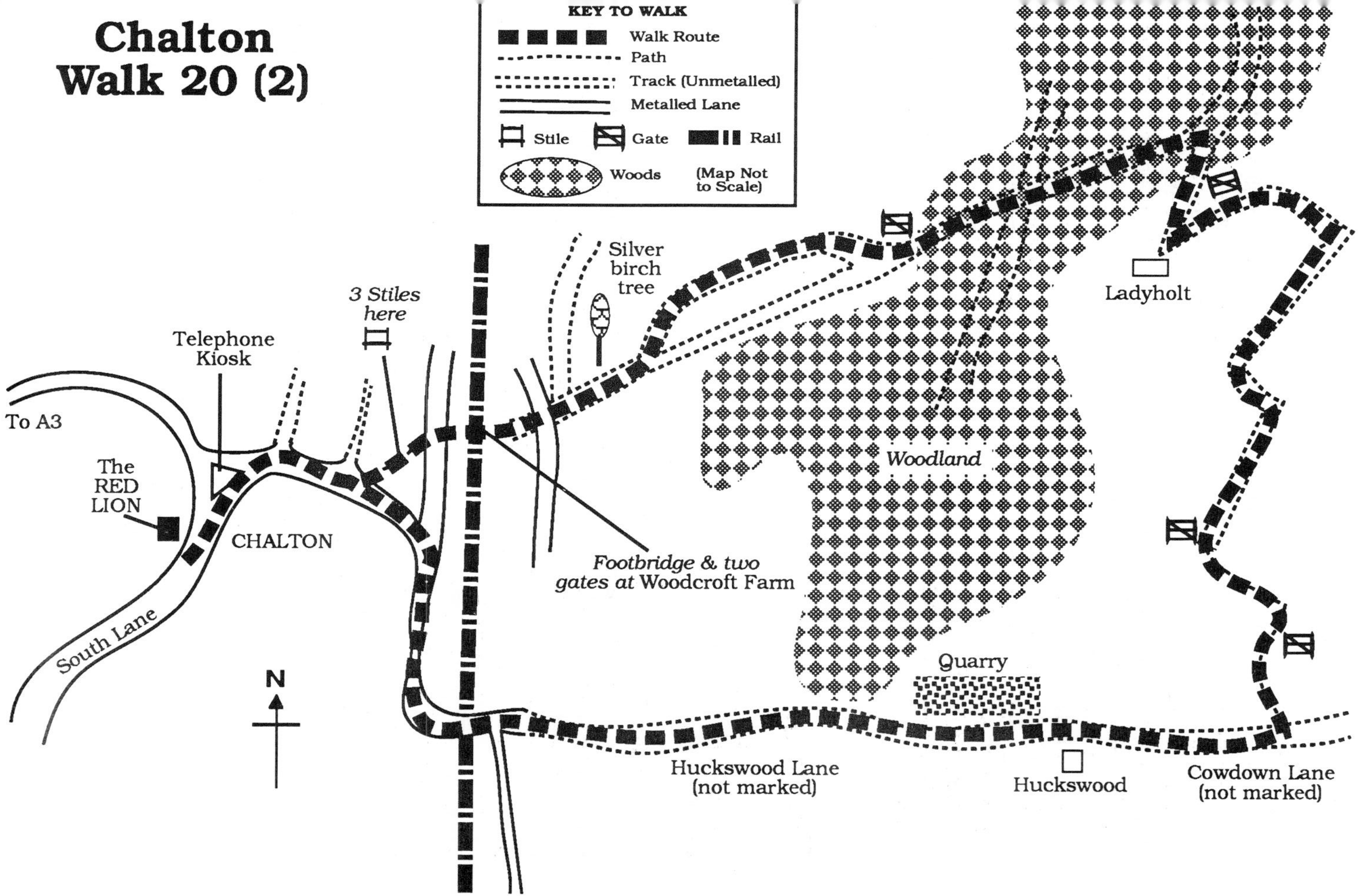

KEY TO WALK

- Walk Route
- Path
- Track (Unmetalled)
- Metalled Lane
- Rail

🚪 Stile ▥ Gate

Woods

(Map Not to Scale)

Cowdown Lane (not marked)

Ladyholt

Huckswood

Quarry

Woodland

Huckswood Lane (not marked)

Silver birch tree

Footbridge & two gates at Woodcroft Farm

3 Stiles here

Telephone Kiosk

CHALTON

The RED LION

To A3

South Lane

N

Gone on strike? St. Michaels Church, Chalton.

going becomes firmer, wider, and easier here. You then come to a wide clearing in the wood where you continue straight on as indicated by the SBP sign.

After about 700 yards you come to a junction of routes – turn right here through a green five-bar gate. Climb up the hill through the coppiced hazels, passing the fingerpost sign on the left, initially turning back and walking parallel with your original route. At the top of the hill turn off left onto the gravelly bridleway. This goes straight for about 200 yards and then veers right by the fingerpost up the hill. Towards the top of the hill the view is excellent to the north and west. At the very top, turn right by the fingerpost sign. Bear left again after about another 300 yards, then right after 20 yards.

As you approach the copse, at the small six-bar wooden gate turn immediately left and walk across the field in the direction indicated by the sign toward the narrow strip of woodland. Go through the trees and through the gate to the field. Walk across this large field and you come to a track where you turn right.

This track known here as Cowdown Lane and further along as Huckswood Lane, is glorious walking and one of my favourite routes in Hampshire and West Sussex. It is clearly an old road that once had more importance than it does now, and connected Compton with Chalton. It is very picturesque, lined on both sides with a good mixture of trees – predominantly beech with an unusual amount of holly. The going is very firm and well drained and would appear to have been built of flints. Positioned by the side of the track is a ruined brick and flint building – close to Huckswood beautifully set amid the downs. Eventually the track gains a tarmac surface and then meets the road. Follow the road over the railway bridge. At this point you have a choice of up and over the hill, or returning to Chalton via the road. As you are probably tired, I have decided to route you back to Chalton via the road rather than straight up the footpath over the hill. Follow the road and it soon brings you back to Chalton and *The Red Lion.*

My thanks are due to Roger and Gillian Riley who kindly tested this walk for me.

21 · A Walk Over the South Downs from *The Royal Oak* at Hooksway

Maps
Landranger 1: 50 000
Sheet 197
Pathfinder 1: 25 000 Sheet
SU 61/71 & SU 81/91
Map Reference of
Start/Finish SU815162

Background to the Walk

This must be the most unspoilt, beautifully situated country pub in the land. It sits, sheltered, in a small secluded valley hidden away from casual passers-by, setting a difficult challenge for the first-time visitor. It is an enjoyable experience, taking coffee outside on a spring morning, listening to the bird song echoing around this wooded valley. Only the occasional rambler passes, on his or her way to the downs.

The *Royal Oak* is around 400 years old but has had many additions (and subtractions). It is the place where Alfred Ainger, one of the most famous Sussex publicans, who became a legend in his own time, spent many many years. Although it seems that everyone who lived within an evening's motoring trip of the pub, seems to have met him, (and can tell the famous story of the toilet which I will relate later), I found little set down on paper until I came across

Pub Facilities
Food is available at most times and in recent summers, afternoon tea has been available. Children are welcome and are allowed into at least one area of the pub. There is a large outdoor area where children may safely play. Dogs are permitted and walkers are welcome to park their cars in the pub car park, providing they patronise the pub before or after their walk. A payphone is available for customers use. The pub serves some very interesting, very strong real ales and has a log fire in the winter. Overnight accomodation is available.

The Royal Oak.

How to get there
Hooksway is situated just off the B2141, seven miles from Chichester.

Bernard Price's excellent collection of articles contained in *Sussex: People-Places-Things*. In this, he recalls meeting Alf Ainger and the information that follows is largely drawn from that account.

Although his speech was of the Sussex tongue, Alf Ainger was originally a Cockney, born close to Bow churchyard. His father moved the family to Worthing in 1887 and survived the fever there in 1893. The family moved to Hooksway in 1905, he married Caroline (Carrie) in 1906 and they took over the pub in November 1907 and held it for over 50 years.

Even in the latter days of the Aingers' reign there were only oil lamps to light the small bar and a small grate, making it a cosy if rudimentary sort of place. On a Saturday night, the pub would be packed by over 80 people and the songs of Sussex could be heard ringing out across the valley.

Due to its close proximity to the West Dean estate, it was not unusual for the occasional royal visitor to drop in while on a shooting trip. King Edward VII visited *The Royal Oak* whilst on a shooting trip as did King Alphonse of Spain. I have also heard that a Kaiser also paid a visit, but I have not found this in print.

He was also fond of telling the story of a 'marriage' in *The Royal Oak*. A man called Page decided that it was high time that a Mr King and his beloved (who were regular patrons of the pub) should get married. In fact he felt so strongly about it that he offered to perform the ceremony himself, for a payment of two gallons of bitter. The couple obviously decided that this was too good an offer to turn down, and Mr Page conducted the marriage with a towel tucked in his shirt collar. "They never had a ring so they just held hands" said Alf "and when it was over they went to live in Black Bush Cottage up on the hill and they was there for years an' they considered they were married".

The most famous of Alf's stories relates to what happened at Midhurst Magistrates Court. Alf Ainger was in the process of renewing his licence for the pub when he was asked about the toilet facilities. His legendary reply was that he considered his facilities adequate enough and said: "But, sir, I have nine acres".

It seems fitting that a pub so full of character as *The Royal Oak* should breed such a well-loved character as Alf Ainger. Even after Alf passed away, Carrie continued to run the pub for a while, putting the seal on one of the longest running pub licences ever. A feat that was recorded in *The Guiness Book of Records*.

These days, the facilities are more modern. There is electric light and both internal and external toilets, but otherwise things have changed little. A good fire is still kept in the winter, and in the spring the lawn blazes with a mass of daffodils. The only sad and surprising thing is that there is no memorial to this famous couple who kept *The Royal Oak* for all those years.

Hooksway
Walk 21

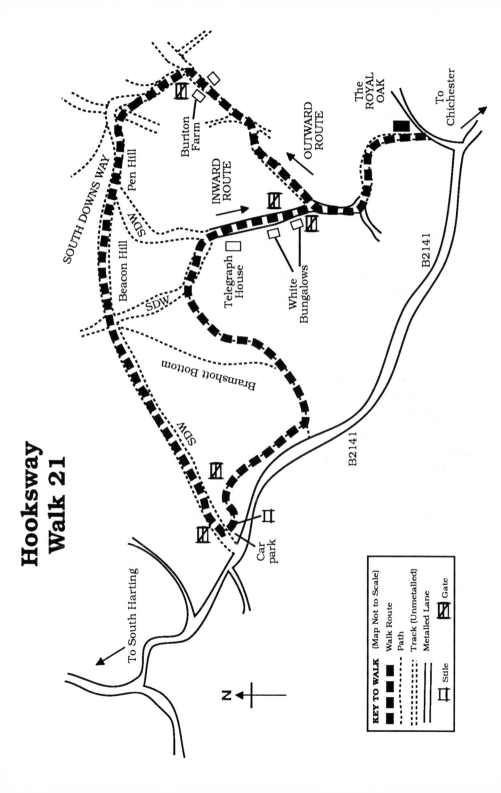

SOUTH DOWNS WAY

Pen Hill

Beacon Hill

SDW

SDW

SDW

Buriton Farm

INWARD ROUTE

OUTWARD ROUTE

The ROYAL OAK

To Chichester

B2141

B2141

Telegraph House

White Bungalows

Bramshott Bottom

Car park

To South Harting

N

*Looking east along the
South Downs Way.*

The late Alfred Ainger.

The Walk

Distance: *Allow 3 hours for this walk;
the distance is 6½ miles.*

From *The Royal Oak* car park climb back up the hill toward the main road. After climbing a fair way up the hill, take the chalky right of way that is angled sharply back on the right. Avoid all deviations off this route until you are at a fork by the white bungalow. Here, take the right-most route – the one without a wooden gate.

Continue on for a further ½ mile, on a route that merrily winds its own way, first descending into a valley, then starting to climb again. Here you are faced with a further choice of routes – again take the right-most lower route. Pass through the farmyard of Buriton Farm and take the next opportunity to turn left, through a small six-bar wooden gate, onto the South Downs Way (SDW), which we are to follow to Harting Hill car park.

Initially our route on the SDW is 'fenced in'. As you enter the copse, continue on the SDW (the left route). Ascend Pen Hill (689 feet) taking the left-most route if you wish to reach the summit. As you descend a few feet from Pen Hill, you are faced with a decision on either deviating from the 'natural' route west which involves a steep scramble up Beacon Hill by the public bridleway, or alternatively follow the official route of the SDW which diverts around the hill, saving an ascent and descent of 160 feet but adding nearly a further mile to your walk. Assuming that you wish to enjoy the excellent views, climb Beacon Hill and then descend into Bramshott Bottom to be faced with two possible routes.

Take the right hand route to continue on to Harting Hill, enjoying the views of South Harting in the valley below. Descend Harting Hill and walk through the wooden gates to the car park, turn left at the fingerpost sign in the car park, following the car park drive for a short distance. As you near the main road, bear left as directed by the fingerpost sign passing the National Trust sign on your left. Climb the stile to take you over the fence and walk for a short distance, at first back toward the road until you come to a short fingerpost where you bear left, away from the road. Take the left-most track that takes you under a yew tree after about 25 yards.

You will be faced with two side by side gates which you should ignore to stay in the wooded area. In fact you follow a route just inside the edge of this wood for just over ½ mile. Although this is an ill-defined path, you will not get lost providing that you keep an eye on the edge of the wood on your left. (Ignore any gates or stiles, without fingerposts that would take you into the field), but follow this ill-defined route through the woods at the edge of the field until you meet a new gate with a fingerpost.

Emerge from this first section of wood and bear half right to walk through the middle of a small copse. At the next fingerpost where we have an open field ahead of us – at this point we turn left. This path swings to the left and then descends amongst some yew trees. You are now at the opposite end of Bramshott Bottom, a lovely isolated spot.

Here, on your left, you will see a dewpond – a somewhat unusual downland feature in these modern times. This experimental project has been built to collect water (mostly from rain rather than dew!) to provide a water source for grazing animals and also a valuable aquatic habitat.

Dewponds have been regularly constructed since the 17th Century, usually in chalk or limestone land where there is usually no surface water. This dewpond became derelict but has now been restored by volunteers from several countryside organisations. The traditional method of constructing dewponds was to scoop a hollow and line it with clay and flints. This modern restoration has used clay plus a waterproof plastic lining underneath and consequently is unable to withstand the wear and tear of hooved animals. Fencing around the pond is designed to keep grazing animals back and a trough has been provided that is fed from the pond.

The ability of these ponds to collect and retain water has interested many writers over the years. Gilbert White mentions a pond near Selborne that "afforded drink for three or four hundred sheep and for at least twenty head of cattle beside" but which was "never above three feet deep in the middle, and not more than thirty feet in diameter". Kingsley Amis in his essay *The Air-Mothers* observed "For on the high chalk downs, you know, where farmers make a sheep pond, they never, if they are wise, make it in the valley or on a hillside, but on the bleakest top of the very highest down; and there, if they can once get it filled with snow and rain in winter, the blessed dews of night will keep some water in it all summer thro', while ponds below are utterly dried up". However as E.V. Lucas points out in his *Highways and Byways in Sussex* the reason for this hilltop placement is essentially practical, as the tops of chalk hills are often capped with a layer of clay, providing essential material near at hand. Richard Jefferies, the countryside writer of Wiltshire and Sussex recorded that "The water has a dead flavour; it is not stagnant in the sense of impurity, but dead, even when quite clear. In a few moments after tasting it, the mouth dries with a harsh unpleasant feeling, as if some impalpable dusty particles had got into the substance of the tongue. This

Buriton Farm – sheltered in a valley of its own.

is caused by suspended chalk, of which it tastes".

There is a choice of two routes at the dewpond – one proceeds straight on following the line of the "bottom" and the other climbs away to the right. Now this route up the hill differs from my 1983 Edition Pathfinder Map – there has obviously been a footpath diversion as the route shown on the map does not now exist. Take the route that climbs away to the right, pass under a telephone wire that serves a very remote place somewhere. Continue following the wide grassy path amongst the invasive hawthorn scrub and you eventually arrive at another fingerpost that confirms that you have arrived at the South Downs Way. Here, turn right and after approximately 700 yards, you leave the South Downs Way, by continuing straight on – the route becomes a public bridleway.

The route around Telegraph House becomes metalled – part of the driveway to the house. By the second white cottage, leave the tarmac drive, by passing through the small six-bar wooden gate and along the right hand side of this small field. You will now find yourself back on your outgoing route and therefore able to re-trace your steps back to *The Royal Oak*.

My thanks are due to Mr and Mrs Chandler and Mr and Mrs Francis, who kindly tested this walk for me.

· BIBLIOGRAPHY ·

This is essentially a book of walks, and therefore the space available for anecdotes and background information is necessary limited. For readers who wish to find out a little more about the history of inns, about Sussex, or about Hampshire, a short list of source material used in the preparation of this book is listed below:

Arthur Mee's Hampshire. Edited by Arthur Mee, The Caxton Publishing Company.

Companion into Hampshire. L. Collison-Morley, Methuen & Co.

The English Inn. J. Burke, B. T. Batsford.

The Guide to Real Ale (Portsmouth & South Hampshire). CAMRA/Ensign.

The Hampshire Village Book. A. Brode, Countryside Books.

Highways and Byways in Sussex. E. V. Lucas, Macmillan and Co.

Inns, Ales and Drinking Customs of Old England. F.W. Hackwood, Bracken Books.

The Place-Names of Hampshire. R. Coates, B. T. Batsford.

Pub Walks in the New Forest. D. Smith, Ensign Publications.

Sussex. E. Meynell, Robert Hale.

Sussex: Customs, Curiosities and Country Lore. T. Wales, Ensign Publications.

Sussex Industrial Archaeology. Edited by B. Austen, D. Cox, J. Upton, Phillimore.

Sussex: People, Places, Things. B. Price, Phillimore.

West Sussex Inns. B. Chapman, Countryside Books.

· ACKNOWLEDGEMENTS ·

Many people have helped with the preparation of this book and I would like to thank all those who have given assistance.

I would like to thank Norman Green for supplying most of the historical information about Hocktide at Finchdean, and David Rudkin and Peter Barge, for the information about Emsworth. Peter Barge also helped with the loan of books.

David Turner and Mervyn Cutten helped track down information on Alfred Ainger (Hooksway Walk, Chapter 21).

Some of the thoughts in the introductory chapter entitled *Pubs and Walking* originated in an unpublished essay: *The English Pub* by Patrick Watts. His kind permission to use this material is very much appreciated.

Keith Whiting of Hampshire County Council Recreation Department answered my right of way queries with his usual efficiency.

A very special vote of thanks is due to all the kind people who helped with checking the walks; their names are given after each individual walk. This activity should provide a very high degree of confidence in the accuracy of the directions and therefore add to your enjoyment.

Finally I would like to thank my wife Veronica who proof read the material and helped out in all sorts of ways.

I would also like to acknowledge the following: Pimlico Books, a division of Random Century (the present publisher), and Peters Fraser and Dunlop for permission to reprint the quotation from *Ha'nacker Mill* from Hilaire Belloc's *Complete Verse*.

Lorena Trigg – for permission to reprint the quotation from *Down a Country Lane* from *Country Spread*.

Mrs M. Homes and Arthur H. Stockwell (publisher), for permission to reproduce the picture of the London to Portsmouth Semaphore from *The Semaphore* by T.W. Holmes.

The photograph of the late Alfred Ainger was reproduced by kind permission from *Sussex: People, Places, Things* by Bernard Price, published in 1975 by Phillimore & Co.

· PUBBERSTAMPING ·

This optional extra to *Pub Walks around Portsmouth and the South Downs* is designed to test your tenacity and thoroughness. To really prove that you have 'done' all the walks, we have with the co-operation of the publicans, (but more on that later) arranged for them to hold a special *Pubberstamp* behind the bar and an inking pad that will allow you to complete the final pages of this book.

The idea is simple, if you have completed a walk then you qualify for the ultimate accolade — that featured pub's *Pubberstamp*. The publicans will no doubt give it to anyone who asks for it but you will have to live with your conscience if you have left out part of the walk or, worse still, used this book as a glorified pub guide and missed out the walking bit altogether! It has to be said that it is a 'very good' pub guide, but even so, make sure you do complete the walk to qualify for your *Pubberstamp*.

So for those who really do complete a walk, they will have a tangible record of their achievement. The following pages are divided into numbered boxes, fill these with *Pubberstamps* in the correct order, from 1-21 and you could win first prize in our competition, namely £100 worth of walking or climbing books. Clues to the correct order for collecting the *Pubberstamps* appear in the text and you must use your skill and judgement to decide in which order you will collect them. There again you could just collect them for collecting's sake and enter the competition anyway. When you have completed your *Pubberstamping* carefully remove pages 127-8 and the back cover and send your entry (the limit is one entry for each copy of the book purchased) to: *Pubberstamp Competition, Ensign Publications, 2 Redcar St., Southampton SO1 5LL.* Closing date for last entries is December 1, 1992.

Please remember that publicans are busy people and you may have to wait around before they can find the *Pubberstamp* and apply it to your book. You may even have to return on another occasion and with the array of fine pubs in this book we don't think that is too onerous a task. Please note that the publicans are helping with this competition on a purely voluntary basis, but obviously we hope it will provide them with new customers in the form of thirsty or hungry walkers. At the risk of repeating ourselves you should always patronise the pub if you use the pub's car park and the same rule applies if you are collecting *Pubberstamps*. But do remember, please do not drink and drive.

1.	2.	3.

4.

5.

6.

7.

8.

9.

10.

11.

12.

13.

14.

15.

16.

17.

18.